Praise for

For some time peop

with a building. Nothing could be further from the truth. In *Bringing Church Home,* Gannon Sims reminds us that church doesn't just happen within the four walls of a church building; church life is present in our families, in our homes, in the ordinary moments of everyday life. This tradition needs to be recovered. Read Gannon's book and bring church home again!

—Winfield Bevins
Director of Church Planting at Asbury Seminary
Author of *Ever Ancient Ever New*

In *Bringing Church Home*, Gannon Sims invites readers to reflect more deeply on the most important and foundational aspects of Christian faith and community. By looking closely and theologically at Christian marriage, Sims illumines Christian practices and understandings for embodying family and community to witness to God's love in Christ for all humanity. This is a wonderfully refreshing and captivating book full of insight, wisdom, and faith.

—Rev. Laceye C. Warner, PhD
Associate Dean for Wesleyan Engagement,
Royce and Jane Reynolds Associate Professor of
the Practice of Evangelism and Methodist Studies

In *Bringing Church Home*, Gannon Sims shares what he has learned from a variety of Christian traditions and provides us with an antidote to the do-it-yourself, privatized version of the gospel that threatens the very life of our churches. He reminds us that the original expression of the church of Jesus Christ is the domestic church. Let us learn from the riches he offers in these pages.

Fr. James Mallon, pastor
Author of *Divine Renovation: From a Maintenance to a Missional Parish*

In our fragmented world of the twenty-first century, many of us experience little overlap between our home and our church spheres of life. Gannon Sims's compelling book *Bringing Church Home* charges our imaginations with a vision of how family life can deepen our experience of life together in the church, and vice versa. Reading this book and taking its message to heart in our local churches will undoubtedly guide us deeper into the rich and interdependent sort of life that God intends for all creation.

—C. Christopher Smith
Senior Editor, *The Englewood Review of Books*
Co-author of *Slow Church: Cultivating Community in the Patient Way of Jesus*

The nuclear family may be the smallest building block of the community, but for most of history families were bigger, including grandparents, single relatives, and friends. Gannon Sims's book presents what he's learned by experience over many years, of the strength and love an expanded family circle can share.

—Frederica Mathewes-Green
Author of *Welcome to the Orthodox Church*

In this creative work that explores the nature of the church through the theological lens of family and familial life, Gannon Sims helps us make sense of deeply personal and richly covenantal nature of Christian community.

Beautifully written.

—Alan Hirsch
Author of numerous books on missional spirituality, leadership, and organization

BRINGING CHURCH HOME

BRINGING CHURCH HOME

How the Family of God Makes Us a Little More Human

GANNON SIMS

Printed in the United States of America

Cover design and layout by Strange Last Name
Page design and layout by PerfecType, Nashville, Tennessee

Sims, Gannon

Bringing church home : how the family of God makes us a little more human / Gannon Sims. – Franklin, Tennessee : Seedbed Publishing, ©2022.

pages ; cm.

Includes bibliographical references.
ISBN: 9781628249446 (paperback)
ISBN: 9781628249453 (mobi)
ISBN: 9781628249460 (epub)
ISBN: 9781628249477 (pdf)
OCLC: 1296153054

1. Families--Religious aspects--Christianity. 2. Families--Religious life--Christianity. 3. Home--Religious aspects--Christianity. 4. Church. I. Title.

BV4526.3.S55 2022 249 2022932873

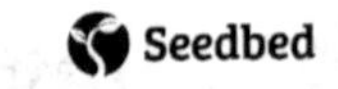

SEEDBED PUBLISHING
Franklin, Tennessee
seedbed.com

Contents

Acknowledgments

My interest and ability to work on this project would not have been possible without an invitation from Tory Baucum and the congregation at Truro Anglican Church in Fairfax, Virginia, who were early pioneers in this work. These friends and partners in the gospel introduced me to Renzo Bonetti, Christopher West, Nicky and Sila Lee, and others engaged in a deeper exploration of the purpose of married and family life. The ongoing teaching and development of curriculum related to Theology of the Body and the work of Bonetti and the Mistero Grande Foundation in Bovolone, Italy, by Chaney Mullins, Hannah King, Alicia Bradford, Brent and Beth Orrell, Tony and Nadia Fraga, and others who have intersected with Truro over the years is a gift to the whole church.

This project has found its way from my head to my heart because I've been able to live it alongside Carey, my bride and coconspirator in our lifelong experiment of self-giving love, and The Center Community in Fredericksburg, Virginia, who often model the gifts of kinship far better than I. This community of mostly young adults and college students has indeed become part of our extended spiritual family. They have been the priests at my elbow and have grown in me a greater capacity to love.

Haley Randall, who lived in our home during the writing of this book, served as an invaluable sounding board and editor on early chapter drafts. Cheryl McCarthy on the Fresh Expressions team undergirded every step of the writing process with prayer. John Upton and Wayne Faison, who head Ascent and the Baptist General Association of Virginia, and Chris Backert, who serves as the national director of Fresh Expressions US, grasped the importance of home and household as we create ways of being church for those the church isn't already reaching. Jason Byassee, my editor, provided some important theological guardrails and challenged me to push further into the subject than I thought I could. This book is a better book because of you. Holly Jones and the team at Seedbed took this project over the finish line with precision and grace. Thank you for helping the dream become reality.

While no project is fully complete and my words will fall short of articulating what I feel deep within my bones, I'm hopeful that the invaluable permission I've been given to learn and to experiment and to write it all down will somehow help spark an increased imagination at bringing church home.

Jesus answered him, "Those who love me will keep my word, and my Father will love them, and we will come to them and make our home with them."

—John 14:23 (NRSV)

Introduction

This book is about how the church is like a family and the family is like a church. It is not a book about family systems or family values. According to the Scriptures, Jesus didn't exactly stop what he was doing when his parents came looking for him. His life upends and reorients both the family system and family values. And that's important for me to say up front.

Before I get too far along, I should probably tell you something interesting about me. I grew up singing in church. First, in my home church and, later, in all sorts of churches. I was as alive and connected to God while singing "Panis Angelicus" with a pipe organ as I was while singing "Right Now Is the Right Time" from a soundtrack by the Brooklyn Tabernacle Choir. When my wife, Carey, and I met, I was a youth leader at a Baptist church on Sunday mornings and a worship leader at an Episcopal church of the evangelical and charismatic variety on Sunday nights. Trust me, knowing those little factoids will help welcome you into my brain.

My comfort with the wider church shapes my understanding of the big family of God and it is what led me some ten years ago to find a home of sorts within Fresh Expressions, a mission movement that started in the Church of England and was later given wings in the United States by the grace of God and the generosity of leaders in the Baptist General Association of Virginia.

Fresh Expressions serves a unique role in the life of the church. We're quite aware of the seismic shifts facing Christianity in the West, and we're building upon the wisdom of the church throughout the ages as we train and equip church leaders to create new (and old) ways of being church today. In the language of Fresh Expressions, we often discuss how we imagine Christian community in various places—first, second, third, and fourth. The first place is the home. The second place is work or school. Third places are restaurants, coffee shops, gyms, or parks. The fourth place is the Internet. While Fresh Expressions has focused on creating new forms of church in every place, this is our first attempt to articulate a theology for and to tell the story of a way of being church that's rooted in home and household.

From the early days of my marriage, I understood marriage as part of my vocational calling. This idea was bolstered through an invitation to work with a group of Roman Catholics who gave me the language to describe marriage as a little church with the same sorts of hopes and dreams we have for the bigger church: that in its engagement in worship, community, and mission, the whole church would be for others and not just for us. This perspective has shaped Carey and me in our work of forming a church community alongside mostly college students and young adults in Fredericksburg, Virginia.

The early church was anchored in homes and the scriptures that begin with a wedding. Genesis 2:18 says, "It is not good that the man should be alone" (NRSV). In the beginning, God walks with and intimately communes with creation. The humans are naked before one another and before God. They are unashamed. There is a holy and beautiful innocence to it all. But it doesn't last.

For much of the rest of the story, God is depicted as the rejected lover and we are the runaway bride. The great drama of Scripture is God's relentless quest to restore things to the way they were at the beginning and more—not because God wills, forces, or demands it, but because God will always be found waiting for us to find our home in him. God wants us to say yes, but only as a willing response. God is jealous, but God is not selfish. If God kept us for himself, there would be no freedom to love.

God is on a mission to woo us. We are his bride. One of the most obvious and overlooked resources for understanding this relationship is the family itself. Healthy families that say yes to God's love create little Edens where we can stand unashamed before God and one another. The family has been instrumental for God's mission all along. But let me repeat: that mission is gathered around Jesus who upends and reorients the family as we know it, pressing us toward the bigger family we have in him.

Too often we've been trapped in the idea of the self-sufficient nuclear family, and this places unnecessary pressure upon too few relationships. This book seeks to address this reality by calling for recognition of the limits within our individual self-sufficiency. As Christian ethicist Stanley Hauerwas wrote:

> Unless marriage has a purpose beyond being together it will certainly be a hell. For it to be saved from being a hell, we must have the conviction that the family represents a vocation necessary for a people who have learned how to be patient. Marriage and family require time and energy that could be used to make the world better. To take the time to love one person rather than many, to have these children rather than helping the many in need, requires patience and a sense of the tragic. Indeed, such activities remind us of how limited we are, but at least we in the Christian tradition claim that it is only through such limits do we learn what it means to be free.[1]

It's ironic that the freedom to open our lives and homes to others is found in our limits rather than in our self-sufficiency. But this is what makes us a little more human. Our limits give us the freedom to be a safe place for others, and the freedom to ask for their help. Opening ourselves and our homes to others and to the light and fresh air that comes from outside takes risk, of course.

---

1. Stanley Hauerwas, *A Community of Character: Toward a Constructive Christian Social Ethic* (Notre Dame, IN: University of Notre Dame Press, 1981), 172.

If we let in others and the light and the air from outside, we're liable to let in some other elements too—but that's how gardens grow.

The renewed understanding of family proposed in these pages promotes the idea of kinship that expands beyond blood ties to indicate mutual understanding and support. That's the essence of chapter 1, where I show this through some of my own experiences of community life with others. Christians place our hope in the blood of Jesus and in the new birth of baptism that announces for all to see that, because of Jesus, the world has been forever changed. The kind of family ushered in by our baptism in Jesus makes possible a different kind of kinship that helps us see a world where there is no us versus them—just us.[2] This kind of solidarity with others—like the whole Christian witness—can seem rather lofty and aspirational at times. It requires patience and imagination, the kind that has sustained the church throughout the cycles of history, which is why it is helpful to ground it within the enduring purpose that marriage and family have played in announcing the kind of radical kinship offered in and through Jesus.

---

2. See Gregory Boyle, *Barking to the Choir: The Power of Radical Kinship* (New York: Simon & Schuster, 2017), 7: "For the opposite of the 'real world' is not the 'unreal world' but the kinship of God. Therein lies our authenticity as people of faith and card-carrying members of the human race. . . . What if we ceased to pledge our allegiance to the bottom line and stood, instead, with those who line the bottom? Us versus Them . . . or just Us?"

Chapter 2 gets into the gritty reality of marriage in daily life and how I've come to celebrate the possibility of marriage both as a form of church and as an echo and image of the divine. In chapter 3, I show how open homes and open lives provide a pedagogy for Christian discipleship. Here, I'll unpack how I've come to practice the presence of God in everyday moments. I'm not going to tell you how to do discipleship in these pages, but this chapter is my attempt to share some stories and some tips.

In chapter 4 I give a brief history of the early church as a segue into how we've come to celebrate worship in our home. How we do church at home invites participation at every level. This model can be used as a way for big churches to deploy their little churches or as a distributed church-planting strategy for people like me who struggle with church-planting strategies. By seeing how every family and household is an expression of church, we are better able to lean into a strategy for growth that fits the natural growth of the family-community.

Chapter 5 speaks to the importance of the table in the worship of the church, at home and out in public. Around the table we get to celebrate until the day when we feast at the great wedding supper of the Lamb. Chapter 6 offers a theological dive into how I've come to understand love, marriage, and the human condition with help from some Catholic thinkers. Through a study of our original state we learn to be a family on mission that is free from guilt and shame and fear.

Chapter 7 challenges us to think about how the household is at the root of economy. Here, I show how the economy of gift where every person is valued helps us learn how God loves. I'll give some examples of how we've been able to spark imagination in our local economy by receiving eggs and espresso and linking up with entrepreneurs. As you read this chapter, consider it your invitation to look at all the ways church and household might take a serious look at economics in your town. Finally, chapter 8 outlines three metaphors used throughout Scripture that are helpful for our journey home. It starts with Jesus, who shows us the way.

Bringing church home is about being at home with ourselves and with those closest to us in the everyday moments of life. It's where making our beds and doing the dishes becomes an echo of the wedding in the garden and where a walk out our front doors and down the streets where we live becomes a foretaste of the city of God. It's a journey where the life of discipleship and participation around the table is so thick with welcome that nobody knows who's the host and who's the guest.

In the pages that follow, you're invited to imagine anew a kind of kinship rooted in family-community love. Using marriage as an example, we'll show how our homes become hubs for mission, pointing toward our true home where we—no matter our previous experiences of family or home or love—can find kinship in God.

"Here I am! I stand at the door and knock. If anyone hears my voice and opens the door, I will come in and eat with that person, and they with me."

—Revelation 3:20

CHAPTER

ONE

Radical Kinship: Shoes and Shared Community

When I finished college, I bought a one-way ticket from Houston to Washington, DC. A few weeks later Wayne and Carolyn Jenkins, two of the pastors at the church I was attending, offered me a room in their home for rent. Their offer was more than a room. What they really did was welcome me into their life.

"I was a stranger and you welcomed me" (Matt. 25:35 NRSV).

A few weeks before my twenty-fourth birthday, I moved from Wayne and Carolyn's into a shared house, an experiment in intentional living, with other young men in their early to mid-twenties. Some were from the US; some were from other countries; and I didn't know any of them. My friends thought I was nuts. They told me I should be moving into my own place. But I was after something different. A friend who thought I was less nuts lent me her copy of Dietrich Bonhoeffer's little book *Life Together*, and told me to go for it. "It'll be difficult," she said, "but it will change your life." In a way, the house functioned in the spirit of Bonhoeffer's community. There were shared meals and shared work. We had simple house rules that were grounded in the Scriptures: *Two are better than one. Be faithful with little things. Don't let the sun go down on your anger. Work for the Lord and not for people. Be reconciled with your brother or sister.* The community house was located on a street where several other families lived in intentional friendship with one another. Some of the homes had basement apartments with lodgers who became part of the extended household. The kids on the street played together and went to school together. We were in and out of each other's homes and each other's lives.

The community house had a couple of designated leaders. Before I moved in, one of the leaders asked me whether or not I felt loved.

"Of course," I said assuredly.

"You'd be surprised how many people aren't able to say that," he said.

When we feel loved, we're less likely to feel like strangers for very long. Why is that? Because we were made for love. Love is the way we're known by others and by God. Love shapes our identity and directs us toward the divine life. In 1 Corinthians 12:31 (NRSV), the apostle Paul calls love a "more excellent way." In the best circumstances we receive love from our family and the friends that grow to feel like family. In the Christian life, these relationships are often found among other Christians, sometimes through becoming part of a local church.

The way we love is easily distorted, however. Most church activities are just an hour or two a week. That leaves so much room for all kinds of other narratives to shape our views of love. In Romans 1:25, Paul noted our proclivity to worship created things rather than the Creator. The Creator is the source of love. Even if we were taught it in church, it's a reality we're prone to forget. Our cultural norms are rooted in self-reliance. This causes us to cut ourselves off from our rootedness in the Creator's love in favor of getting by on love of our own design. Rather than receiving love, we either hide from it or control it for ourselves. When that happens, it's as if the windows of our souls have been closed and the blinds shut to keep ourselves from seeing the light. St. Augustine called this *incurvatus in se*—"an inward turn." When we turn inward, we begin using love selectively, usually as a way of getting what we want—finding ourselves in ourselves while keeping others at arm's length or using them to meet our needs.

True love is quite the opposite—it's a free and generous outward act. It's a call out of hiding and away from control to a place where we're able to *give* ourselves to others rather than using them to get what we want. One of the hopes of this book is that we would be able to reorient and rediscover the way of love as it is intended by the Creator. In this way the windows of our souls that were previously shut are opened and flooded with light. The windows of our souls are not unlike the windows of our homes, of course. If our windows are open, our souls are more likely to be opened as well. If others are invited into our homes and our lives, we're less likely to live turned in on ourselves and more able to gaze at the world anew, spurred along the most excellent way by a caring community as the Creator first intended.

We belong to God and to one another, but so much of what we read and look at pushes against that claim. There are entire courses and channels created with the aim of helping us find ourselves outside the context of lived community. One article called out the "empty religions of Instagram," noting the ways that social media influencers have been allowed a position of moral authority in the lives of their followers without ever addressing the deeper question of "What we should believe in beyond the limits of our puny selfhood?"[1] The article contends that celebrity influencers may peddle in secrets of living your best life but aren't chiefly concerned with "the best use of your life."[2] How could they be? Those who know me best know that I'm a big believer in knowing who we are. But at the end, we can't really know who we are without knowing *whose* we are. We need daily reminders of this from others who actually know us to help us live into this reality.

In his book *Engagement with God: The Drama of Christian Discipleship*, the Swiss theologian Hans Urs von Balthasar suggests that many of us are on a quest for our own *individual* identity but that we often mistake individualism for *isolation* or *privacy*. Privacy is turning

---

1. Leigh Stein, "The Empty Religions of Instagram," *New York Times*, March 5, 2021, https://www.nytimes.com/2021/03/05/opinion/influencers-glennon-doyle-instagram.html.
2. Ibid.

inward. Privacy says, "leave me alone! Let me do my own thing." But in the Christian view, "the world is no longer an anonymous collection of [private] individuals . . . the light of heaven penetrates through Christ and the Church into the darkness of the world, so it visibly gives personality to the whole human community."[3] Von Balthasar likens this to a leavening process. While the world is prone to distort our view of love, training us in a form of individualism rooted in private isolation and a form of community rooted in collective tolerance, Christ is the leaven that helps us become fully individual in genuine shared community. In the light, we become a person. In the light, we discover what it means to be human. Jesus—the light of the world—is both fully human and fully divine. He takes our need for privacy and our quest for self-help and bathes it in the waters of baptism where we discover who we are in light of who he is. From there, we begin pulling back the layers of who we think we are or thought we were to discover our true identity in true community. Community in the best sense means that our individual contributions aren't simply tolerated but treasured, sometimes challenged and always refined in light of the greater whole.

In shared community we find unity in distinction. This is true freedom, and it is what Jesus comes to bring. In true community we find constant companions who acknowledge our distinct characteristics and gifts.

---

3. Hans Urs von Balthasar, *Engagement with God: The Drama of Christian Discipleship,* trans. R. John Halliburton (San Francisco: Ignatius, 1975), 34–35.

Then, in community, this acknowledgment allows us to be called higher and nearer to the sacred heart of Jesus. Without a true identity blessed and ordered by Jesus in shared community, the search for self leads to private isolation and loneliness on the one hand or control, attention-seeking, and people-pleasing on the other. It pulls us into the quicksand of misbegotten and inwardly focused identity where we think that no one really sees, cares, or understands.

While I'm not sure I could have named it at first, an experience of shared community was what I was looking for when I moved into the shared house. In my head, I'd worked out the ideal community, but I needed to really live it. It took a few months, but I finally and clumsily took to heart Bonhoeffer's warning that people who loved their *idea* of community more than the community itself would actually destroy the community.[4] In the house we learned that love was for others. This love, as we'll learn a bit later, was a costly kind of love. It was a fight-it-out (even when you were tired and just wanted to go to sleep) kind of love. This love shaped and transformed a small group of young men who had very little in common other than the meals and chores we shared together.

One didn't even have to be a confessing Christian to live in the house. You just had to learn the five little Bible verses and you had to participate in the daily meals, work, and discussions. I later learned that these simple principles framed what monks and others living in intentional

4. Dietrich Bonhoeffer, *Life Together*, trans. John W. Doberstein (New York: Harper & Row, 1954), 27.

Christian community often call a *rule* or *way* of life.[5] Because they felt a sense of belonging in the community, several of the guys set aside their atheist or humanist or skeptical tendencies and began reading and later living out the gospel. Life in this house made the world look a little bit more like the kingdom of God.

On Monday nights we had our house meeting. For the first few minutes, we discussed the chores for the week. Who would clean the toilets? Who would sweep the floors? Then we moved on to matters of our relationships with one another. How were we doing? We asked each other if anyone had anything they needed to confess. If they were holding a grudge or needed to discuss a miscommunication or to apologize for anything, no matter how big or small, this was the time. The meeting wasn't over until we'd dealt with our issues.

Then, after an awkward pause, someone would apologize for something small like leaving their laundry in the dryer. We had an unwritten rule that anyone who found someone else's laundry in the dryer would remove it from the dryer and fold the clothes that were left inside. It was a simple pay-it-forward kind of gesture and it all but ensured that perfectionists in the group never left their clothes in the dryer ever again.

One evening during the house meeting these two guys from Benin needed to work out a disagreement they

---

5. One of the earliest and most universal of these is The Rule of St. Benedict, composed in 516 by Benedict of Nursia. Adaptations of this rule are still in use in many monasteries and Christian communities today.

were having. So they argued with one another. In French. Only the guy from Lebanon would have had any clue as to what they were talking about. It felt like an eternity, but eventually they worked it out. If there was anyone at our house meeting that night who needed to short-circuit their proclivity to flee a good old-fashioned conflict, that was the night to stay in it; to witness an argument, and to see it end in peace.

I shared a room with one guy who got annoyed with me because my shoes were left beside my bed. When he stumbled over my shoes in the middle of the night, he didn't wait until our next house meeting to bring it up. He woke me up right then.

"Gannon, I need you to wake up," he said.

I was startled, groggy, and more than a little bit annoyed.

"Huh?"

"Gannon, I need you to put your shoes away."

"What's going on?"

"Wake up, I need you to put your shoes away."

"Bro, are you serious? Don't you have bigger things to worry about? I mean, there's ethnic cleansing going on in Albania, and you're worried about my shoes?"

"Gannon, I'm your roommate. Don't talk to me about Albania until you pick up your shoes."

After I got out of bed and put my shoes away, we went downstairs to the living room to talk. At the end of these kinds of conflicts, even if they were small, we always offered and received the words of forgiveness. A cool, "No worries, I'm good," never sufficed. We had to say the words: "I forgive you."

"Will you forgive me?"

"Yes, I forgive you."

In that moment, I had been given grace mediated by Christ through a friend who cared enough to help me deal with something as small as my shoes. I'm glad he did.

I took with me what I learned in that house and the others before it and have attempted over the course of my life—imperfectly, of course—to live out the gospel in every other house in which I've lived.

What about your house? What if your desire for love moved beyond your own self-interest to the interest of others? What if your desire for love wasn't repressed, but able to be fully disclosed and ordered within a community of healthy relationships? What if the way to love was rooted within a family or family-like community that turned each one's desires outward because they were so transfixed on and transformed by God's love? What if this way of life transformed the church because we began to realize that this kind of love is what it actually means to *be* the church? In a day where church is no longer at the center of society, what if this kind of family-community love overflowed from our living rooms into our neighborhoods, schools, and workplaces where we would begin to see a glimpse of heaven on earth?

It starts when we learn to put our shoes away.

The pages that follow are about how the church can become more like a family and the family more like church by reframing and recovering the radical kinship of shared community life, where there is no *us* or *them*, but just *us*. Here, we'll show how the family and family-like community—concepts that have been sentimentalized by some and politicized by others—can be reoriented. When we do that, we can help people experience the love of family who have never felt it before.

In the Scriptures, we read how kinship is shaped by Israel's experience as slaves in Egypt: "Remember that you were a slave in the land of Egypt, and the LORD your God brought you out from there with a mighty hand and an outstretched arm" (Deut. 5:15 NRSV, cf. 15:15; 16:12; 24:18, 22). God reminds Israel not to forget their past. Because of this, space was made for the continuous revaluation of Israel's kinship ties where the stranger, the fatherless, and the widow were welcome. Israel's history as slaves in Egypt and the "invoking of the kinship of fellow sufferers is meant to motivate Israel to offer the kind of hospitality that she herself longed for during her exile in Egypt [cf. Deut. 10:19]."[6] Because of this, Israel's idea of kinship is reoriented to enfold the stranger into their house and within their gates. They were taught to welcome the stranger because they were once strangers themselves. They had to remember not to forget.

Throughout my life I try to remember not to forget. I remember the time I bought that plane ticket and moved halfway across the country. I remember the people I barely knew who gave me a roof over my head and welcomed me into their life and into their family.

Over time, Israel forgot they were strangers. The practice of a revaluated kinship that included the

---

6. Mark R. Glanville and Luke Glanville, *Refugee Reimagined: Biblical Kinship in Global Politics* (Downers Grove, IL: InterVarsity Press, 2021), 38.

welcome of outsiders lessened. By the time Jesus arrived on the scene in the first century, Israel had clearly defined limits as to who was in and who was out. "A first-century Israelite would have considered any Gentile or Samaritan to be completely beyond the pale, not even *registering* as acceptable to God (Mark 7:24–30)."[7]

This is the context with which Jesus brought his own message to Israel. And it got him killed. Jesus disrupted the family. For him, kinship and family ties depended on those who did the will of God (Mark 3:35). While some whole households aligned themselves with the way of Jesus like that of Mary, Martha, and Lazarus, still others of Jesus' followers left their families to become part of Jesus' new reordered family where they "found their first kinship with Christ and with the divine Father and then with each other."[8]

There's a reason why some Christians call one another *born again* and other Christian traditions consider the baptism as a holy symbol of new birth. Radical kinship in Jesus means that we die to our selves and our family identity and rise again in solidarity and mutual agreement with a family and community identity that is reoriented around communion with Jesus within the larger family of God.

This line of thought requires a reordering of our life. To get here, I had to live it and I had to get my own house in order. I had to wrestle with the purpose of my marriage

7. Glanville and Glanville, *Refugee Reimagined*, 75–76, emphasis added.
8. Ibid., 77.

and my home. Radical kinship isn't just something I experienced as a twenty-something. It's something I'm trying to live with intention every single day. It's been twenty years since my first experiences of kinship with a family and community I barely knew, but those experiences remain instructive for my own understanding of the household. I have no other choice. Ten years into my marriage it became painfully clear that Carey and I were unlikely to have children of our own. The multiple medical consultations and procedures left us with few answers. At the time we were in the midst of our own Egypt. Our only solace was the hope of a reoriented identity around the kind of family Jesus desired to bring. We needed to learn how to care for others like family because family was what we needed most.

One evening at home after reading through the book of Ruth—another biblical story of kinship transcending blood ties—Carey put a basket outside the front door of the little brick rambler where we lived as a symbol of our emptiness. She asked the Lord to *fill the basket.* In the story of Ruth, Naomi, Ruth's mother-in-law, had lost her immediate, nuclear family and had returned from the region of Moab to the town of Bethlehem where she and her husband were raised. She asked her friends and distant relatives who were present there to refrain from calling her by her given name and to call her *Mara,* which translates "bitter" instead. "I went away full, but the LORD has brought me back empty" (Ruth 1:21a).

At the time, Carey and I were bitter and burned-out. In the midst of our struggle with infertility, we'd buried ourselves in the work of ministry. I was helping launch the new Fresh Expressions US movement while we were simultaneously redeveloping and pioneering new ways of being church on a college campus. We had lots of permission from our denomination but little local support. Five years into this new ministry venture, not only were we feeling empty in our personal struggle, we were feeling empty spiritually as well. If we were going to continue in what we were doing, we needed God to fill the basket.

As we prayed about whether or not to make our exit, the Lord sent us a couple of Ruths—two twenty-somethings named Faith and Luke—who pledged to be in the struggle with us. They were from a charismatic Christian background and gave us what they believed to be a word from the Lord. They told us that they felt we would be spiritual parents on the college campus and for young people in our city. This is not a word they took lightly. Over the next few years, that word would unfold before our very eyes.

We loved our little brick rambler. It was just a mile and a half from the university, but we'd longed to live closer so we could better integrate the rhythms of the collegiate community into the rhythms of home. After lots of searching and multiple meetings with our Realtor, we'd cast that bread upon the water. After resolving to stay in the rambler and a couple of years after their word, we found a house a block from campus and across the street from several of the college students and young adults in our budding church community. We renovated the attic of our new home and soon it became lodging for Haley, first as a graduate student and later as a first-year high school teacher. When Haley got married and moved out, she and her husband leased a nearby apartment big enough to share with one of their single friends.

The nature of our household and neighborhood community life might be too radical for some and not nearly radical enough for others, but it's significant for my calling to a different understanding of the household. For us, we have no other choice than for our home to be a place of openness and welcome, a place of grace in the midst of devastation. Otherwise, our marriage might have turned in on itself. Along the way, kinship ties and spiritual children we didn't plan have cropped up because we were running on empty and we asked the Lord to fill the basket.

The older I get, I realize the beauty and limits of my own partiality. When I was young, I was taught I could do or be just about anything. While I'm not one to give up on dreams, the fact is I will never be lots of things. I can only be who I am. So rather than focusing on what or who I'm not, I try to stay focused on who I am in light of who God is. It may sound simplistic, but so is the nature of the radical kinship to which I aspire. It's not rocket science and I can't say exactly how it might take shape in your own life. All I can say is that by accepting my limits, I've found a clearer path toward a very old way of following Jesus alongside others of similarly limited abilities who are trying to do the same.

I choose to live this way because it helps me remember where I've come from. I remember the way I was raised by parents courageous enough not to stop me from buying that plane ticket from Houston to Washington, DC. I remember that when that plane touched the ground,

I was a stranger in a strange land who had hospitality extended to me over and over again. I remember being enfolded into a family who was different from my own. I remember the joys and pains of singleness and childlessness, and every day I try to remember not to forget.

Questions for Reflection

- Do you feel loved? If so, how do you share your experience of love with others? If not, how might an experience of shared community help with this?
- One of the hopes of this book is that we would be able to reorient and rediscover the way of love as it is intended by the Creator. What do you need to let go of to open yourself more fully to God's love?
- This chapter touched on the idea of unity in distinction. How are you learning to acknowledge the distinct gifts and abilities that you and others bring into your experience of community? How might you allow those in your community to call you beyond yourself into a fuller Jesus-shaped identity?
- Unity in distinction means acknowledging our limits. How does acknowledging your limits help you live a richer, fuller life?

Therefore a man leaves his father and his mother and clings to his wife, and they become one flesh.

—Genesis 2:24 (NRSV)

CHAPTER

TWO

The Great Mystery: Why Marriage Means Planting a Little Church

It was quiet when we arrived. The glimmer of candlelight reflected along the chapel's frescoed walls drew our attention beyond ourselves. The quiet of the chapel's interior gave us a greater sense of our own interior, somehow beckoning us toward the eternal. Instead of taking a seat, most of the worshipers entering the chapel took to their knees. The sight of a room full of people on their knees brought me to my knees as well. A few minutes before seven o'clock, a young man walked toward the front. Situating himself between the statues of Mary and Jesus, he picked up a guitar and began strumming a familiar tune. We were at a Catholic retreat center near the town of Rorvereto in Northern Italy, but the tune was a contemporary worship song made popular by an artist from Texas. My first thought was—*Wait, what?* My second thought was—*Wow.* As the people began singing

Grande sei, grande sei, il nostro Dio, in a hushed tone, somewhat under my breath at first, I began singing too, but in English.

How great is our God.

Carey and I were thousands of miles from home, but we were closer to home than we thought. We'd ventured to Italy for our work with Fresh Expressions to learn from the leaders in a network of more than three hundred home gatherings—an initiative called *community family evangelism*. We wanted to learn more about how the family is an expression of church. I'd been to evangelism conferences (I was raised in a Christian tradition steeped in evangelism), but I'd never seen anything like this. We were there to get practical, to learn how this worked and how to apply it with our team back in the US. After several days of meetings, my head was as full as the pages of my notebook. By the time we started singing, my head gave way to my heart.

How great is our God.

How great is our God who meets us and continues his revelation on our hearts and in our flesh? How great is our God who continues his revelation on the hearts and in the very flesh of each and every human being? Many have called the church a sign and a wonder. The church is a living demonstration of who God is and what God does. The health of the church is directly determined by the health of the relationships within it.

When I was growing up, my family was incredibly active in our church. We were there every time the doors were open, and we were often the last ones to leave. As a family, we thought our role was to be involved *in* church, to volunteer *at* church. But I'm not sure we were ever taught that we *were* church.

But what if every home that declares the greatness of God could really be a little church? Carey and I get to do a lot of counseling with young couples preparing for marriage, and I often tell these couples that we're preparing them to plant a church. Think about that. Every couple preparing for marriage is preparing to plant a little church. This gives us a greater imagination about what marriage is for. The church is only a sign and a wonder because the believers who make up the church are also a sign and a wonder. Every married couple serves as a visible and tangible symbol of the reality of God's great love. They are a window or icon into the eternal. In a day of changing culture and declining church attendance, many are attempting to fix the church. But what if we're starting in the wrong place? How can we fix the bigger church when we haven't yet understood the reality of the little churches we should have been planting all along?

We can't fix the church until we realize the marriages that are so foundational for the little churches that make up the whole church are first designed to fix us.[1] Nothing shines a light on who we are in the way that a husband or wife or family member does. Families push our buttons. They know the stories that make us laugh and how to make us cry. Every family is different. Your experience of family is different from the person sitting next to you, but

---

1. Renzo Bonetti, *Signs of Love: Christian Liturgy in the Everyday Life of the Family*, trans. Alessandro Sona and Brent Orrell (Franklin, TN: Seedbed, 2017) further unpacks this concept.

imagine the power of the body of Christ when it is fortified one person, one marriage, and one family at a time. If marriages are strong, families are strong and the whole body of Christ is strong.

The work of fixing or restoring the church from this foundational place is costly. There's no work-around. It starts from within by allowing God and those closest to us to shine a light in the deepest recesses of our lives and it moves out from there as we allow others to tell us what they see in us that's beautiful and what they see in us that needs refining. As we give way to this patient and sometimes painful process, the people and situations that God places in front of us give us life and make us more whole than we were on our own. It gets back to the idea of unity in distinction.

As we sang of the greatness of God in the Italian chapel that night, Monsignor Renzo Bonetti, the organizer of the conference and leader of the Mistero Grande Foundation, offered a way forward for the global Christian witness by giving us a glimpse of the garden. He showed us how our theology applies to our body. The marriage relationship highlights the obvious physical distinctions of the body, but it goes much deeper than this. Our distinctions make us who we are, but most often become apparent in our interactions with others. The depth of his words penetrated our hearts. As he finished his message, he begged us to learn how to see.

"Look into the eyes of the people who are seated around you," he said. "Really learn to see. As you look into their eyes, pray for their eyes to become the eyes of Jesus."

I noticed an older man just behind me. Many of those gathered were seated with their husband or wife, but this man was seated alone. Our eyes met. And I prayed for him. I later learned that this man had lost his wife some years ago and that the community of people brought together through Don Renzo's foundation was a place that helped him continue living out his vows to her in a greater way. Despite the fact that his wife was no longer living, this man was more in love with her than ever before. The love and commitment he had for his wife was pulling him toward a greater love.

Bonetti continued: "Now look into the eyes of your husband or wife. See them with the eyes of Jesus and pray for their eyes to become the eyes of Jesus." I'd gazed into Carey's beautiful brown eyes so many times. I knew these eyes. They were the window of her soul. But I had never before prayed to see her with the eyes of Jesus or for her eyes to also become the eyes of Jesus.

Bonetti went on: "Take the hand of your husband or wife. Remember the day you stood before God and spoke your wedding vows. Pray together that these vows would be renewed in your spirit."

"Now when you're ready, walk the aisle together as bride and bridegroom and come forward to receive a blessing."

These sorts of reflective practices are a hallmark of Bonetti's work. Times of worship, including a special time of Eucharistic adoration, occur every evening at every conference hosted by the foundation he leads. The practice makes contextual sense. In Catholic teaching, Jesus is embodied in the sacrament of the Eucharist

(Holy Communion, the Lord's Supper). The bread of the Eucharist is a visible reality of the presence of Jesus. So, the practice of gazing upon the bread of the Eucharist teaches us to see Jesus. In the sacrament of marriage, the couple is a visible sign of the presence of Jesus. So, the task in marriage is learning to see and be seen. This is a mysterious and humbling proposition. It's a cross worth carrying and it's a mission worth dying for.

As Carey and I walked forward in the chapel that night, Bonetti prayed a blessing for our marriage and gave us a bar of handmade soap wrapped in tissue paper and tied with string. At every service of Adoration, Don Renzo always offers a gift.

"When you wash your hands with the soap, it will give itself for you," he said. "It will give you its aroma. It will purify you and make you clean. This is how it is with Jesus. Jesus gives himself for you. He gives you his aroma. And he will make you clean."[2]

Jesus makes profound things simple, the crooked straight, and the rough places plain.

Don Renzo used soap as an illustration to exhort married couples and to echo the words of the apostle Paul, who used marriage as an illustration to exhort the church:

> Husbands, love your wives, as Christ loved the church and gave himself up for her, in order to make her holy, by cleansing her by the washing of water by the word so as to present the church

---

2. My notes from the service of Eucharistic Adoration, Regional Community Family Evangelism Conference, Rorvereto, Italy, June 27, 2014.

> to himself in splendor, without a spot or wrinkle or any thing of the kind—yes, so that she might be holy and without blemish. In the same way, husbands should love their wives as they do their own bodies. He who loves his wife loves himself. For no one ever hates his own body, but he nourishes and tenderly cares for it, just as Christ does for the church, because we are members of his body. "For this reason, a man will leave his father and mother and be joined to his wife, and the two will become one flesh." This is a great mystery, and I am applying it to Christ and the church. Each of you, however, should love his wife as himself, and a wife should respect her husband. (Eph. 5:25–33 NRSV)

John Paul II says the appeal to the beginning, the appeal to the human heart, and the appeal to the final resurrection are essential for our interpretation of Ephesians 5.[3] As we're learning to interpret this passage from the apostle Paul, it's helpful to know what Jesus teaches about marriage. When Jesus was questioned on divorce by the Pharisees, he appealed to the hardness of their hearts, saying that it was not this way in the beginning, back in the garden of Eden (cf. Matthew 19; Mark 10). Two other teachings of Jesus are also worth noting.

The first is his teaching on adultery from the Sermon on the Mount. For Jesus, the outward act of adultery has

---

3. John Paul II, *Man and Woman He Created Them: A Theology of the Body*, from the introduction by Michael Waldstein (Boston: Pauline Books and Media, 2006), 466.

its roots within our interior life. As in his teaching on divorce, Jesus' greatest concern is the condition of the human heart. He says that any man who looks lustfully at a woman has already committed adultery—in his heart. And, presumably, vice versa. No one decides to commit adultery out of the blue, of course. That decision stems from lots of other little decisions. Jesus is drawing a boundary here. "Don't go near adultery," he seems to be saying. "Don't even give it a look."

The second teaching is found in Matthew 22. In first-century Judaism, there was a debate between the Sadducees and Pharisees about what happens when we die. The Sadducees believed that the soul went to Sheol. Nothing more. The Pharisees believed in the resurrection from the dead. In an attempt to disprove the resurrection from the dead, the Sadducees asked Jesus about marriage in heaven. Jewish law mandated that if a brother died and left his wife without children, one of his brothers had to marry the widow. The Sadducees then wanted to know which of the brothers the woman was married to at the resurrection. Jesus, cutting through their attempted argument, said that there is no marriage at the resurrection. At the end, we will not be married in the sense natural to us. We will only be married to God.[4]

Jesus calls his opponents beyond their own objections to consider another way. In each of these texts, Jesus uses the language of the body to address human relationships. In his teaching on divorce and adultery, he appeals

---

4. Matthew 22:30; Mark 12:25; Luke 20:35–36 as referenced in John Paul II, *Theology of the Body*, 466.

to the heart. In his teaching on the resurrection, he says that marriage in the earthly sense pulls us into a greater way of thinking about marriage in the heavenly sense. This bolsters the apostle Paul's appeals to the marriage relationship—as a mystery and metaphor. Marriage is not somehow better than other relationships. But it is a distinct picture for the way Christ loves his people—the church—and a foreshadowing of what will be when the church is at one with God.

From the teachings of Jesus to the great mystery of marriage found in Paul's writing, a far greater case is made for the direction of our life than the kind of life that so many of us are content to live. These teachings are not concerned with the bare minimum—what must I do to inherit eternal life? These teachings point beyond the bare minimum of law and action and human institution to ultimately show that life is about the condition of our heart, our heart's response to God's heart, and how that leads to a life lived for others.

Marriage is a vehicle that God has placed in the world to point us and those around us toward Jesus—the way to God's heart. At the end, the marriage vehicle will fall away just like everything else, but until then, marriage and all of the relationships influenced by your marriage or my marriage or your parents' or your friend's marriage contains within it the possibility to transform society from the inside out.

With a firm understanding of Jesus' appeal to the heart—and to the fact that human marriage is not the final act—let's look back at Ephesians 5, to an often-misunderstood teaching from Paul: "For the husband is the head of the wife as Christ is head of the church, his body, of which he is the Savior" (v. 23). Christ is the head—and the church is the body. This metaphor is lived out in the marriage relationship with the husband as head and the wife as body. This metaphor gets a lot of bad press. It's been misinterpreted as oppressive and it's also, sadly, been used to oppress. But let's think back to the give and take, the unity in distinction. Have you ever seen a head function without a body? Or a body function without a head? Paul calls marriage *the great mystery* not because it is oppressive, but because it speaks to a level of *interdependence* in the same way that we see interdependence in the life of God. The only act of subordination here should be that of "the sinfulness of [our] own humanity to the powers that flow from the mystery of the redemption of the body."[5] Our relationships are mediated through Jesus, who is making all things new.

American culture has very few categories for interdependence. Indeed, the role of the community and the individual has been the subject of much debate.[6] Americans are prone to prize and even idolize independence. We revel in the narrative of the cowboy, the mystique of the lone ranger. We're taught from a very early age to pull ourselves up by our own bootstraps. It's

---

5. John Paul II, *Theology of the Body*, 428.

6. For a fuller illustration of this debate, see Collin Woodard's *American Character: A History of the Epic Struggle between Individual Liberty and the Common Good* (New York: Viking, 2016), 57–85, and Kristin Kobes Du Mez's *Jesus and John Wayne: How White Evangelicals Corrupted a Faith and Fractured a Nation* (New York: Liveright, 2020).

a remarkable legacy. The American dream gave birth to a strong work ethic and eventually—despite our complex and disastrous history of slavery and racial injustice—opportunities for many to achieve a measure of financial success no matter who they are or where they came from.

The same kind of individualism has crept its way into our religious life too. My grandfather used to tell me that religion was a private affair between a man and his God. This view was shaped more by the culture of the European Enlightenment than by the community life of the triune God. Even the parts of America founded on a more communitarian way of life have historically held private or individualistic views of God. This leaves many of us exploring spirituality on our own.

This yearning we discover in our faith journey isn't a private affair. It's rooted in a web of dynamic and interdependent relationships; this is even more pronounced in the marriage relationship. Bonetti calls the marriage relationship a "Trinitarian greenhouse" for how God loves. While the first humans hid from God, it is very difficult to hide in a marriage. It forces us to see ourselves at our best and at our worst. As we open our hearts to another and as we invite Jesus to show the way, we are strengthened and conditioned for love. We learn the shapes of the little church in three dimensions: *up, in*, and *out*.

Made for Worship—The Upward Dimension

When Carey and I got married, we chose some ancient language for use in our wedding vows that has shaped our practice of generative life. "With this ring I thee wed, with my body I thee worship, and with all my worldly goods I thee endow." Our whole life together is an act of worship and a practice of giving and receiving love as an echo of the God who is love. Bonetti fears this dynamic part of the relationship—the whole of married life as an act of worship—is in danger of being lost, because it's not being taught. More often than not, in the church, the pastoral care of the couple centers around premarital counseling. There may be a weekend retreat or a small group, but rarely is there any other development for the couple unless the marriage hits a crisis. Clergy and pastoral staff who are typically the first line of defense on such matters—faced with the crisis of shrinking budgets and church attendance—are often "overwhelmed by problems that feel more urgent than the needs of the family."[7] By shifting our understanding of marriage preparation as preparation for planting a little church, we put the worship of God at the core of the relationship. By teaching couples that they are an icon or window into the way God loves, and that their life together bears fruit in the lives of others, we have the building blocks that show how marriage can be a solution for the church rather than another momentary crisis for clergy.

Worship means *to ascribe worth*. The life of the couple is meant to be lived so that every gesture, word, or action toward our spouse is an opportunity to ascribe worth to God. Together the couple helps call one another higher as they learn to see one another through the eyes of Jesus and as they are beckoned by Jesus into the divine life of God.

---

7. Bonetti, *Signs of Love*, 4.

Learning to See—The Inward Dimension

I'm not sure it was love at first sight, but I definitely remember the first time I saw Carey. She was seated near the back of a Sunday evening young adults gathering at The Falls Church in Northern Virginia. After a few sightings, I finally introduced myself. That conversation gave way to dating and an eventual pronouncement of our love for one another. While our love for one another continues to grow, our love is not just *for* us. It is larger than either of us can contain, because love is a visible sign pointing toward God and the now and not-yet reality of his kingdom. But as I learned in the chapel that evening in Rorvereto, we have to keep learning to see.

Learning to see one another—from the facial expressions we make to the ways we encourage, judge, or dismiss one another—is valuable practice for life. It causes us to ask ourselves why we react to the other in the way that we do. We can only learn to see one another in the right way when we learn how God sees us. This gets back to identity, of knowing *whose* we are. When we know the source of our identity that comes from God, we have a better sense of how to walk in relationship with another. In relationship, we learn to see one another as God sees. A helpful question, posed by marriage and family therapist Harry Dunne, is this: "What is it like being married to me?"[8] This question creates space for us in two ways. First, it allows us space to do our own soul searching. What

---

8. Harry P. Dunn Jr., *One Question That Can Save Your Marriage* (New York: Putnam Publishing, 1991).

is it like being married to me? The only person we can change is ourselves. Because there are continents within our interior life that have yet to be evangelized by God's love, we must spend the necessary time with ourselves to know what we're really like and then how our actions are reflected back to others. This question isn't meant to drive us toward being reclusive, isolated, or selfish. It's to help us articulate our own unique individuality so that the great mystery of marriage can be more fully experienced far beyond just us.

Second, we use this question to reflect upon how we experience the other. It takes all the practice and vulnerability we can muster to articulate and hold a mirror to our spouse. Reflecting back is not an exercise in being petty or judgmental. It's a way of training ourselves in the here and now for the way we believe things will be at the end when everything is made new, and every relationship is subsumed by the wholeness and fullness of God. When we share how we experience the other, we create room in ourselves to receive the good and the bad. It builds our confidence, strengthens our foundation, and is bolstered by our mutual recognition that Jesus is present and ready to render aid. As we ask this question of ourselves and each other, we also ask it of Jesus. What *is* it like being married to *me*? As we give ourselves to Jesus and one another, we again recognize that to love rightly, Jesus must consume all of us. He is the object of our devotion, the location of our affection, and the one to whom all worth is ascribed. While we will never achieve anything in this life that comes anywhere close to what is really possible in the love that God reveals in Jesus, if we can position our heart to receive just a fraction of his heart in our relationships with one another, we can make a good start. Then we'll see our homes becoming a little more like the home we will make in him.

Again, while the marriage relationship is foundational, it is not a kind of first-class status. Many Christians have gotten things backward on this point and this has led to some misperceptions. Remember that Jesus was single and so was the apostle Paul. In 1 Corinthians 7, Paul actually says that he wished that others could remain single.

I often find that my single friends and family members often have a much greater capacity to give and receive than those of us who are married. My sister is single. She's got a great gift for planning adventures and making good food. On a Saturday morning it's not uncommon to find her out on her bike delivering breakfast burritos filled with homemade chorizo to all her friends.

Called to Fruitfulness— The Outward Dimension

Whether we are married or not, all of us are made to generate life, to be fruitful and multiply. We can all ask the question of those closest to us: What is it like to know me? To experience me? Our ability to articulate the role we play in the lives of others enables us to express our unique individuality and how that individuality enhances and gives life to others. The most literal way of giving life, of course, is through the married couple as they give birth to and raise children. Not all of us are able to have children, of course. That's why fruitfulness is a mandate for every person to practice in our work, creative pursuits, and in our care for others. Bonetti says that when we learn to love like God loves, we play the role of mother and father to every person we see and every child we meet.

Many of us had people in our lives in addition to, or even besides, our parents who showed God's love to us. As you reflect upon your life, consider the people in your life that generated life in you. What were their names? How did they show their love? In the same way, what projects and other creative endeavors are you or your family involved with that generate life?

As the couple becomes the little church, we see the upward, inward, and outward dimensions displayed in their lives together. All of this helps move us toward our final destination—our ultimate union at home with God. In the next chapter, we'll see how the home is a school of discipleship preparing us for that ultimate home.

Questions for Reflection

The Upward Dimension

- How is our life together an act of worship?
- How is our home a place of worship?

The Inward Dimension

- What is it like being married to me?
- What is it like to know me as a friend?

The Outward Dimension

- How are we practicing fruitfulness in our life for others?
- How might our household become an expression of church and a haven for pastoral care, discipleship, and mission?

Hear, O Israel: The Lord *our God, the* Lord *is one. Love the* Lord *your God with all your heart and with all your soul and with all your strength. These commandments that I give you today are to be on your hearts. Impress them on your children. Talk about them when you sit at home and when you walk along the road, when you lie down and when you get up.*

—Deuteronomy 6:4–7

CHAPTER
THREE

Unhiding Talents: Everyday Discipleship

I'll never forget the time I first laid eyes on Bertha: the twelve-foot Christmas tree nestled into the bay window at the big house on Forest Avenue. Tony, Nadia, their four kids, and Tony's godmother, Nanci, giggled as they told us about the voyage to the farm and their decision to topple this magnificent tree. Their giggles turned to outright laughter as they remembered carrying, hoisting, wrestling, and lassoing the behemoth to the top of their minivan for the twenty-mile journey home. After several failed attempts at getting the gigantic fir through the front door, it was finally placed in its designated spot. At once, the heavy-duty tree stand displaying all the benefits of German engineering sprang into action, forming a secure claw-like grasp around the base of the trunk. The tree, the base, the story—all of it—was excessive. And wonderful. Sort of like Christmas.

That night under the glow of the twinkle lights and the sparkle of ornaments, we were in awe. Both the grandeur of God's kingship and the kindness of God's friendship were on display in the conversation and laughter around this oversized evergreen.

There is something about the love of the family and the gravity of a home. At their best, families and the homes they inhabit can be and do what nothing else can. I'm sure you've seen a Christmas tree the size of Bertha displayed in a mall or a hotel lobby, but I doubt you felt at home there.

Tony and Nadia embody the joys (and struggles) of a household that functions in a web of extended family-like relationships. Their parents were part of an ecumenical Catholic community that has its origins in the Christian renewal movements of the 1970s, so from an early age they were accustomed to the notion of kinship ordered around Jesus. Tony's parents shared their home with Nanci, a close family friend who became Tony's godmother. When Tony and Nadia got married, they moved into the townhouse community where Nanci was living. Their own faith was renewed as a young married couple, in part, through their relationship with Nanci, and soon the three of them began volunteering with area youth and sharing their small townhouses with high school and university students. After several years, Tony and Nadia began looking for a larger house nearer the university that better fit their mission. The only problem was that the neighborhood near the university was out of their price range. So, Tony and Nadia started praying and Nanci started praying with them.

Not long after they started praying, Tony and Nadia found *the one.* Nanci was with them when they saw it for the first time. It had a big front porch, an open kitchen, and a finished basement—perfect housing for university students. But the price was far too high. So Nanci made a proposal. The house wouldn't be out of their price range if they were willing to share. Nanci wasn't planning on making a move, but she asked whether or not they might consider buying and owning the house as an intentional commitment of their life together reordered around Jesus. Together, they made an offer, got a contract, and moved in later that year. Nanci got the master bedroom, Tony and Nadia picked the next largest room, and their four kids piled into one room so they could have a spare room for guests. For a season, five university students shared the two rooms in the basement, making life beautiful for twelve people and one Betta fish all under the same roof.

Their home became a little monastery. They said prayers together each morning before school and work. They set ground rules and shared responsibilities for shopping, cooking, and cleaning. Every Friday night, they ate a meal together at a full table with the household and extended friends and family. They invited their neighbors: university students and the family who ran the cleaners nearby. Nadia tells a story about a visit from a young South African girl who was living in the area and working as a nanny. It was a typical Friday at home. Tony was making dinner. Nadia had some laundry to fold upstairs, so she invited the young woman up for a visit while she folded. Nadia thought nothing of it, but the young lady was deeply moved. Her job as a nanny meant folding lots of laundry, but she had never imagined being invited into this family's personal space to watch someone *else* fold the laundry. Sharing the ordinary is such a simple thing. But it opens up worlds.

Hospitality

This is what hospitality is all about. If we're going to create environments where there is no *us* or *them*, inviting someone into your laundry room is a pretty good place to start. To be free of shame, we need to be willing to be seen as we fold our laundry. Hospitality in the truest sense blurs the line between host and guest. A true guest is put at ease. They're welcome to help. They know where the dishes are. They learn the household rhythm and they're okay with the clutter that remains a normal part of life. Hospitality is different from entertaining.

When Wayne and Carolyn offered me the basement room in their house, they assured me that if dinner was on the table, I could join them. Their friends became my friends, and my friends became their friends. We read books together, worked puzzles together, and I learned not to interrupt Carolyn while she was watching *Jeopardy*. I remember a time when some of their relatives were coming from out of state for a spontaneous visit. It was a Saturday around lunchtime. Wayne stopped his yard work and, before we could blink, he'd pulled out the china and started setting the table. Carolyn got on a step stool, reached into the back of the cupboard, and found a few cans of oyster stew. "We'll doctor it," she said. It happened in a flash, but there was no hurry. When the guests arrived to find the table set with a simple salad, oyster crackers, and piping hot soup, it was as if they'd walked into a lunch date that had been fixed on the schedule for months. I caught this way of hospitality from being around Wayne and Carolyn because hospitality, like many things that matter in life, is more caught than taught.

One day my colleague Shannon Kiser asked a group of leaders we were training to think of all the lessons we'd learned in life: "How many of you signed up for laundry study before you learned to wash your clothes? Did you take a class on how to have a first date before you had one?" We learn how to do lots of things through trial and error. The same is true for hospitality.

When Carey and I moved to Fredericksburg, Virginia, we bought a little brick rambler in a 1950's neighborhood. At 960 square feet, it was all we could afford within a couple miles of the university community we were called to serve. The upside was that the house had a partially finished basement that ran the full length of the house. My brother-in-law encouraged us to turn the finished part into a dining room. He called it "the dining cave." We bought two ready-to-assemble tables on sale at a big box store. My friend Gregg helped me put them together and, before long, we had seating for twenty. I put the overhead light fixtures on a dimmer switch, unrolled a piece of burlap, and placed six candlesticks down the center of the table. Once we dimmed the lights and lit the candles, we were transported from a 1950's basement with white cinder block walls to what Celtic Christians might call a thin place. Even a simple meal around that table gave us a foretaste of the wedding supper of the

Lamb. While the marriage of heaven and earth is present in every place, in a thin place it becomes more apparent somehow—like an epiphany. An epiphany is an illuminating discovery or a sudden revelation or manifestation of the divine. There's a Christian holiday called Epiphany. It happens on January 6, at the end of the Christmas season. We celebrated Epiphany (and other holidays that don't get much notice) around that table. Epiphany is the celebration of the star that appeared over the place where Jesus was when the Magi brought gifts to Jesus. It's also a celebration of Christ's baptism and first miracle. While we've found that it's hard to squeeze in one more party or event into most people's schedules before December 25, our friends are nearly always free around Epiphany. At these parties we talk about what Christ's Epiphany means and we discuss the events in our lives that we've found particularly illuminating.

Tony and Nadia couldn't have known the impact their Christmas tree would make on us. Wayne and Carolyn didn't expect those cans of oyster stew to be put to such good use. I never imagined the symbolism or the epiphanies we'd have around that massively long table in the basement. Each of these stories represents a moment of unity in distinction explicitly showing how the great mystery of marriage is lived out every day. It's the everyday moments that build the life of Christian discipleship.

The Life of Discipleship

The first conversation about Jesus I remember having was at McDonald's with my mom. I was probably four or five at the time. Every week my mom and I went to McDonald's on our way to the grocery store. We would split a Happy Meal and talk. My mom's first conversation about Jesus was with her grandmother, a devout Methodist, who taught her to memorize the Twenty-Third Psalm from a needlepoint that hung on the wall in her bedroom.

What about your first conversation about Jesus? Who were your influences along the way? Outside of my parents, I had the good fortune of being influenced by "a great cloud of witnesses" (Heb. 12:1), most of them at the First Baptist Church in Conroe, Texas, where I was baptized at the age of eleven. I went to Sunday school, joined the new Christians class, and later joined the youth group. When I got to the seventh grade, Pamela, one of our youth ministers, told me I was a leader. She pulled together a group of four or five of us for weekly conversations about God and she taught us how to have daily devotions, "a quiet time," she called it. She taught us how to share our faith and how to give talks at a breakfast group we had before school at 7:00 a.m. In high school, these early morning gatherings were held at McDonald's in hopes that our friends who wouldn't come to church might meet us there.

Then came the day when our pastor retired. Not long after that, Pamela was called to be the youth minister at another church—a good move for her. By the end of that year, all but one member of our pastoral staff had moved on to new places of ministry. Soon it became apparent just how much our church relied upon paid staff for our spiritual development.

Hindsight is 20/20, of course, but what if the central organizing principle of our church were the families that made up our congregation rather than the programs orchestrated by church staff? What if these families had been challenged, developed, and organized in such a way so they saw their home and family life as a solution to the problems—not just in the church community—but in the city and society as a whole?

This way of organizing the church might look something like this: the pastor recruits a few married couples with a natural inclination of sharing their home and family life with others. These are the families who throw parties and host the youth group. They're the ones who already know their neighbors. Through the pastor or other staff members' intentional mentorship and spiritual direction, these families and their households become hubs for mission and extensions of the congregation. In some cases, these homes and families might form the backbone of a more decentralized way of being church. When the realities presented by the COVID-19 pandemic hit, this is exactly what our little church community started doing. We'll unpack this possibility for lightweight, home-based worship in the next chapter.

Most church leaders I know spend a lot of time and energy coming up with new initiatives and programs for the members of their church. Many Christians I know sign up for these programs or at least think they're supposed to. The programs come in a variety of forms: classes, seminars, and small groups, often with a lecture-based format. In this format, the teacher plays the role of expert. Everyone else listens. They nod along. Sometimes they respond to a question or comment proposed by the teacher. The teacher is active, the participants passive. That's how it goes week after week.

These aren't the only programs or initiatives offered through the church, however. There are service projects. And mission trips. And music ministry. All of it deeply enriching and rewarding. But activities or programs organized once a week or once a year are not enough. Christian discipleship is not simply learning information *about* Jesus or doing things *for* Jesus. It's becoming *like* Jesus in apprenticeship with others who are committed to doing the same. Apprenticeship is a lived reality. It's learning from the way that Pamela taught us to lead the breakfast group at church and applying it back into the laundry room at home.

Acknowledging the Presence of Christ

How might you consider the kinds of actions that are most often found *at church* and bring them into your little church? In his book *Signs of Love: Christian Liturgy in the Everyday Life of the Family*, Renzo Bonetti shows how the family displays the visible presence of God through simple acts and gestures in the home. These simple acts and gestures are derived from the kinds of ceremonies and practices we might learn in church. Bonetti uses the word *liturgy* to describe what he's after. That word is most often associated with corporate acts of Christian worship, usually in churches that are considered more historic or formal.[1] But even the most informal church gathering has a corporate liturgy. Bonetti wants us to consider how these corporate patterns of worship are instructive in the everyday moments of life.

Think about your home—the physical structure that houses your domestic church. What liturgy or regular rhythm do you find there? In our home, whoever wakes up last makes the bed. Sometimes it's a race to see who gets up first. If it's a tie, Carey and I make the bed together. In the home, our bedrooms are a sort of an inner sanctuary. They are places where we experience the deepest experience of intimacy. Some church buildings have a dedicated place for kneeling, often near the altar or Communion Table. In the home, that place for kneeling is often at the bedside. During seminary, Carey and I served at an Anglican Church that gave great attention to the details of the liturgy—from the way we entered the church to how we knelt before Communion and folded the linens at the altar table. Every time I make the bed, I fold the quilt across the foot. For some reason, when I do, I remember Gloria Mullins, who was a sort of spiritual mother in that church. Her prayer life—she taught me to pray the Rosary—coupled with an impressive attention to detail with things like altar linens made a permanent

---

1. Writing from the Eastern Orthodox perspective, liturgical theologian Alexander Schmemann calls the liturgy "a corporate act in which the whole Church, i.e., the entire community, is involved, in which it really participates." *Of Water and the Spirit: A Liturgical Study of Baptism* (Crestwood, NY: St. Vladimir's, 1974), 8.

impression on me. For some reason when I make the bed, I'm often led to pray for that congregation.

In that same church, there was a crucifix over the altar. Years ago, we hung a crucifixion scene on the wall in our bedroom. It's a simple piece crafted by an artist in South Sudan given to us as a gift by my supervisor at the State Department when I left government service for seminary. It wasn't until Bonetti caused me to think of our bedroom as a sacred space that the gravity of the scene and its significant place in our bedroom became obvious to me. When we rearranged the room in our current home, we hung the scene directly over the bed. Truthfully, it's the most practical place for it—but it makes an impact on us every morning when we make the bed. On the opposite wall is a painting of a church building Carey bought from a street artist in Ecuador—it had hung on the wall in our room for years, but it also has a renewed significance. In the corner of our room is a fiddle leaf fig tree. It's a trendy plant that we do our best to keep alive. It's also a reminder of the garden and a visible challenge for our little sanctuary to be free from the fig leaves that played a part in humanity's first experience of sin and shame.

Just inside the front door of that Anglican church where we served, stood a baptismal font filled with water. As we came and went, we touched the water with our fingers, making the sign of the cross as we did. First we touched our forehead, then our heart, then across to our left shoulder, over to our right shoulder and then again back to our heart. It took me a few weeks to embrace this practice because it is outside of the tradition in which I was raised, but once I learned that it served as a way to remember my baptism, I caught the significance and embraced the practice. In baptism we die to our old way of life and are raised to new life in Christ (Rom. 6:4). When I remember my baptism, in a sense I'm dying to my old way of life and even my old suspicions about other kinds of Christians. I'm doing so as an act of worship and a sign that baptism is a physical marker of my primary identity in Christ.

After making the bed, my next stop is the bathroom sink. After I turn on the water, I cup my hands. As the water fills and overflows my cupped hands, I wet my face three times in the name of the Father and of the Son and of the Holy Spirit. Then I remember the words that were spoken over me at my baptism: "Buried with Christ in baptism, raised to walk in newness of life."[2]

In that church, the liturgy began with an opening hymn and a dramatic procession of people in robes led by someone wielding a thurible filled with incense. My daily procession is far less dramatic. I grab my running shoes and head toward the incense of freshly ground coffee. Coffee is the incense of our home. As I breathe it in, I make my cup, then I feed the cat and while it's still quiet, I light a candle, and turn to prayer.

Bonetti says that the resurrected Jesus is more alive than we are, and it is he who stands as the heart of the

---

2. During the COVID-19 pandemic, the practice among Christians of praying the Lord's Prayer or singing the Doxology during handwashing had such an influence that some of my friends' children won't wash their hands without praying or singing.

domestic church. The domestic liturgy, he says, "is any gesture and word that consciously expresses the presence of Jesus. He is in the center of the spouses' lives, both for them and their children, who are aware that they are all one with Jesus."[3] On paper, this all might come across as neatly packaged and rather sanitary. It is not, of course. Acknowledging and developing the liturgy of the home takes time and intention and great levels of flexibility depending on the day or season of life. We can be disciplined, but we can't be too rigid about this. You may be into the idea, but your kids might not be. Take it all in stride. In our liturgy, we were able to appropriate our experiences in a church that places a great emphasis on routine gestures to guide the physical appropriation of our home as a little church. What has been rewarding about learning how to think about our home in this way is how our regular routine has become a conscious acknowledgment of the presence of Jesus in each of these simple acts without adding another event to our schedule. Making the bed has become a reminder of the altar, washing our face is a reminder of baptism, the smell of coffee of the aroma of Christ (2 Cor. 2:15). Simple acts like feeding the cat and taking out the papers and the trash have become conscious acknowledgments of our responsibility as stewards of creation. This is how it looks to live the life of discipleship in the actions and gestures we take up every day. The liturgy of the church

3. Renzo Bonetti, *Signs of Love: Christian Liturgy in the Everyday Life of the Family*, trans. Alessandro Sona and Brent Orrell (Franklin, TN: Seedbed, 2017), 24.

then helps shapes the pedagogy—or way of teaching—in the home. This is how our bodies and, ultimately, our lives are shaped for worship and discipleship.

My friend Dave Male serves as the director of discipleship for the Church of England. He reminded me once that the word *disciple* doesn't appear in the New Testament outside of the Gospels and Acts. In the rest of the New Testament, the church had to grapple with how to *follow* Jesus *without* his physical presence. That's why the apostle Paul uses gestures and actions to illustrate how to follow Christ. He tells us to put *on* Christ,[4] be *in* Christ[5] and again to submit to each other out of reverence *for* Christ.[6] It's why the New Testament gives us the language of armor, clothing, and athletic training to show us how to inhabit the way of Jesus. It's why the marriage relationship is an enduring symbol of God's generative, self-giving love and why the little gestures of everyday family life are effective vehicles for this message.

Asking Good Questions

The future of humanity passes through the family as does the future of our faith.[7] We must be ready, as the

---

4. See Romans 13 and Galatians 3. Colossians 3 includes the language "clothe yourselves with compassion, kindness, humility, gentleness, and patience" (v. 12), showing how language shapes our actions and intent.
5. 2 Corinthians 5:17
6. Ephesians 5:21
7. John Paul II, *Familiaris Consorito*, accessed January 2022, Vatican.va, 75.

apostle commands, to give an account for our faith: "But in your hearts revere Christ as Lord. Always be prepared to give an answer to everyone who asks you to give the reason for the hope that you have. But do this with gentleness and respect" (1 Peter 3:15). Some translations use the words *meekness* and *reverence* instead of gentleness and respect.

At the beach, my five-year-old cousin once asked me why the ocean was so big. It had been a while since I'd been confronted with the quandary—and beauty—of five-year-old questions, but my best response in the moment was: "What if the ocean is so big because it helps us understand that God's love is that much bigger?" The intonation I used during my response, THAT. MUCH. BIGGER. surprised even me. I responded to my cousin's question with a question. Like a rabbi.

> In the Gospels, Jesus was addressed as rabbi; and a good rabbi knows how to ask great questions... [The] Jewish rabbinical study approach was not about cynicism, skepticism, or doubt. Instead, it was about cultivating curiosity and awakening wonder in a mysterious yet accessible God, who is known more deeply through questions rather than mere answers. Jewish thought believes the deeper the questions, the deeper and richer our awareness of God. For without wonder, there would be no questions.[8]

---

8. J. R. Briggs, doctoral dissertation, "The Development and Testing of a Curriculum for Inquiry-Based Leadership in the

Disciples of Jesus are steeped in the language of Jesus. Jesus told stories and asked questions to make his point. So should we.

My colleague J. R. Briggs spent an undergraduate semester in Jerusalem. He tells a story about a rabbi who assigned him a biblical passage—the binding of Isaac in Genesis—and told him to pair up with a friend and to come back the next day with one hundred questions about that passage. That assignment changed Briggs's life. Briggs said:

> Jewish theological education is shaped significantly by questions . . . Yeshivas (Jewish Schools) often engage in what is called *chavruta* (meaning "friendship" or "companionship") where students pair up, read a sacred text together, and discuss and debate its meaning and implication almost entirely through question-asking, not giving answers. . . . Rabbi Michael Skobac, director of education and counseling for Jews for Judaism, shares: "Questions are the very lifeblood of what it means to live as a Jew."[9]

The practice of asking good questions is essential for our discipleship. Within the family-community, we should be safe to ask any question.

Ecclesia Network for the Advancement of God's Mission" (Philadelphia: Missio Seminary, 2019).

9. Ibid.

Living the Word

The Discovery Bible Method[10] is a simple and replicable way to help understand and live the Bible in groups of three to five people. This process helps people get comfortable talking about the Scriptures and sharing the story of Scripture with others. There are many adaptations of this method, but at the heart, there are five basic moves:

- What do I like about this passage?
- What does it say about God?
- What does it say about me?
- What am I going to do about it?
- Who else needs to hear this story?

Over time, asking these sorts of action/reflection questions shapes our lives, our families, and others. As we become comfortable sharing the language and stories of Scripture with others, we and one or two others might begin a new group with a couple of people who are unfamiliar with the Bible. Over time, this group might start another group. Parents can try this with their children. Their children can try it with their friends. Parents can try it with their friends or with others who might consider them to be their spiritual parents and so forth. Through inquiry-based learning, people begin sharing the stories and living the language of Scripture. We'll look at a

10. Discovery Bible Study was developed by David L. Watson and Paul D. Watson and has been adapted by a number of Christian organizations. Learn more at www.contagiousdisciplemaking.com.

similar way of reading and praying through Scripture in the next chapter.

Learning to Pray

Craig Williams, a Presbyterian pastor in California and a voice of wisdom on the Fresh Expressions team, says the invitation to discipleship is simple: "It's be with me, being with Jesus." By being with others who are engaged in *being with Jesus*, the language and actions of the faith become instinctive. They're like second nature. Nowhere is this more evident than in the language of prayer. I'm the most with Jesus in my daily prayer. Daily times of private prayer in the early morning are water for my soul. I do my best to invite others into this daily practice. Our community joins in thirty minutes of prayer three mornings a week. We've had seasons where several of us have prayed in person, and other seasons where we've joined together online. Either way, it's a regular opportunity to be with Jesus together.

In my daily prayer, I often use the *Book of Common Prayer* or the *Liturgy of the Hours* to help guide my practice. For several years I was in a setting where I participated in a form of morning prayer where we used the same words nearly every day. In our current setting, our life with others often takes shape around newer believers, so my preferences for ancient language can sometimes be a barrier. In this context, I've learned to let go of my preferences in favor of keeping it simple. Because the language and concepts from my years spent in more formal times of morning prayer have gone from my head into my heart, the language of ancient texts including the Psalms usually guide me without me ever having to read directly from a book.

In our community, morning prayer is a simple version of an ancient form often including a psalm, a moment of silent introspection, a time of thanksgiving, and a time of extemporaneous prayer for the needs around us. In this simple liturgy, we create space to say "sorry," "thank you," and "please." More formal settings might label these moves confession, thanksgiving, and petition. The goal of these morning prayer times is to allow prayer to guide us all day as we seek to engage and invite others into the practice.

Mike Breen's simple Christian discipleship process works very effectively around opportunities to pray with and for others. Like a rabbi or sensei training their student or a medical resident shadowing a physician, Breen deploys a fourfold move: I do, *you watch*. I do, *you help*. You do, *I help*. You do, *I watch*.[11]

Imagine that someone you're getting to know is having a bad day and you want to cheer them up. You're out running errands with one of your kids, so on your way out of the store you buy some flowers as a gift for your new friend. You deliver the flowers and when you do, you also offer to pray for them. Your child observes all of this, and you talk about it on your way home. The next time something like this happens, you ask your child if they want to help pray for the person when you deliver the gift.

---

11. Mike Breen, *Building a Discipling Culture* (Pawley's Island, SC: 3DM Publishing, 2016), 139–55.

Over time, the child develops some instincts around this. The next time their friend needs cheering up, your child would take the lead and you the parent might help—and eventually watch.

The family is a great gift to the world, Bonetti says. "The real danger for families today is that they live this gift in privacy, like a hidden talent (Matthew 25:1–20) . . . this thwarts the family's mission to share Jesus."[12] Bonetti shows how, from the outset, our lives in Christ were never meant to be hidden or private. "A true family is one who opens its doors; shares its love with the world and in so doing, creates a family of God that transcends time. The creation of this larger family shows both the roots and the destiny of the individual and the family itself."[13] Again, the way of discipleship doesn't always require another event on the calendar, just intention in everyday life. The fourfold move isn't merely about learning a task; it's about creating a culture of curiosity where we notice what's going on in our midst and allow it to shape our calling to others.[14]

When we envision our homes as little churches, they become hubs for community and mission in the everyday. We often think of the Great Commission in Matthew 28 as a calling to go and make disciples in far-off places. But the call of the Great Commission is an "as you go" calling for everyday discipleship and disciple-making no matter

12. Bonetti, *Signs of Love*, 36.

13. Ibid., 29.

14. I'm thankful to my colleague Tim Lea on the UK Fresh Expressions team for this insight.

where we live. The text essentially says, "while going into all the world . . . make disciples of all nations . . . baptizing . . . and teaching them to obey all I have commanded" (Matt. 28:19–20, paraphrased). That means when we put on our shoes in the morning and leave our little church for work, school, or errands, we do so with the intent of noticing others and making disciples as we go. While driving onto the interstate, we drive *in* Christ. We learn to be *in* Christ while checking e-mail or making deliveries. It doesn't take a long or prescriptive time of prayer with our family before we go out to accomplish this. It just takes intentional acknowledgment of the simple fact that our lives are designed to be a blessing to others while we're going into the world. And it's all the better if we go two-by-two.

One Saturday, Carey and I were out for a walk and we ran into our friend Veronica at the farmer's market. Veronica is the mother of a newborn and a toddler and she was having an experience typical of young parents, juggling a stroller, a newborn, a toddler, and a bag of groceries all at the same time. It was clear that she needed help getting back home so we walked with her, taking turns pushing the stroller and greeting neighbors along the way.

In his book *The Domestic Monastery*, Ronald Rolheiser, a Catholic mystic and head of the Oblate School of Theology in San Antonio, Texas, recounts a tradition prevalent among spiritual masters, "that we will not advance within the spiritual life unless we pray at least an hour a day privately." His opinion about this changed after being confronted by a mother of young children.

"As it is, I gave her different advice: 'If you are home alone with children whose needs give you little uninterrupted time, then you don't need an hour of private prayer daily. Raising small children, if it is done with love and generosity, will do for you exactly what private prayer does.'"[15] Raising children, he insists, is deep soil for the spiritual life. It is a drawing away from the world to another, perhaps less selfish, way of life that requires "the bringing of oneself into 'harmony with the mild.'" This sort of harmony with the mildness of a sleeping infant or in the midst of the infamous two-year-old's temper tantrum provides grounding for a life of continuous prayer "perhaps more than the monk or the minister of the gospel, she [the mother] is forced, almost against her will to mature."[16] Parents learn that their time is not their own. We can all learn something from parents and the perspective that parenting brings as the doors of our domestic life draw open to the world.

As I mentioned earlier, Carey and I do not have children of our own, so our journey has required a certain grounding in prayer of a different sort. It is in encounters with friends like Veronica and others like her that we see how our expression of the domestic church—often with more bandwidth than a domestic church facing the demands of young children—intersects in simple ways that allow a collective sharing in God's love for the world.

---

15. Ronald Rolheiser, *The Domestic Monastery* (Brewster, MA: Paraclete Press, 2019), 9.
16. Ibid., 13.

My friend Kevin prays with his kids whenever they leave the house. One night after dinner his family wanted popsicles, so he and his young son drove to the grocery store. Before getting out of the car, Kevin and his son prayed together. As they prayed, they got the sense that someone in the store was experiencing pain in their knee. They asked God for help finding this person. On the way to the popsicle aisle, Kevin's son noticed a stock clerk unloading a box of canned goods. "Excuse me, sir," he said, "this might sound strange, but are you experiencing any pain in your knee?" The clerk said that he wasn't. There weren't very many people in the store that night so after asking everyone he could find whether or not they had a hurt knee, Kevin's son was a little discouraged. But Kevin had another idea. He went to the customer service desk and asked the store manager if she'd be willing to make an announcement over the public address system. She agreed. Over the intercom the store manager asked for anyone in the store with a hurt knee to report to the customer service desk. After a few awkward minutes, a store employee walked down the aisle from the employee break room toward the customer service desk. "That's her!" Kevin's son exclaimed. "There she is!" The employee hadn't even heard the announcement, but when they asked about her knee, she confirmed that she was indeed experiencing chronic pain, so Kevin's son asked if he and his dad could pray for the employee's hurt knee.

It doesn't always happen this way, and I'm not sure exactly how this works, but when Kevin and his son prayed, the store employee experienced immediate pain relief in her knee all because a father and son made the life of discipleship part of their late-night trip to the grocery store.

What if Kevin and his son hadn't found the person with the hurt knee in the store that night? They would have gone home with popsicles but not with the story of healing. Would their act of faith have been any less important? Of course not. As Christians, we take risks to live what we believe to be true. We—like Jesus—appeal to the heart and the longing for God that resides within every person. The posture of our heart propels our actions. The results are outside our control. All we can do is make the choice to act from a pure heart rooted in love for others. This is the freedom we receive in God and it gives us the opportunity to keep on asking, keep on seeking, and keep on knocking no matter the results (see Matthew 11; Luke 7).

Giving and Receiving Freely

Christian freedom is as countercultural as it is habit-forming. "The teachings of Christ are at the heart of the Christian's counter-habits, and they must be embodied."[17] Justin Martyr (ca. 100–165), a participant in a Roman house church and a well-known teacher, apologist, and disciple-maker, placed great emphasis on living like Jesus. He went as far to say that those who

---

17. Alan Kreider, *The Patient Ferment of the Early Church: The Improbable Rise of Christianity in the Roman Empire* (Grand Rapids: Baker Academic, 2016), 144.

spoke the words of Jesus but didn't live the ways of Jesus weren't Christians at all.[18]

The earliest Christians were almost always Jewish or had at least some knowledge of the ethics and habits of the Jewish faith. While the Jewish faith wouldn't have been totally unfamiliar to many in Roman culture, it wasn't a dominant influence. As the Christian community spread throughout the Roman Empire, there became a need for the early Christians to adapt to their context. Apart from its Jewish roots, the Christian way of life was viewed as out of step with the dominant culture. Roman culture was pagan. There were many gods and ritual cults formed to serve those gods. The rich were highly acclaimed. The poor were often forgotten. The Christian way of life—shaped by equality and patience; forgiveness and love—offered a different way forward, but the average Roman would have needed significant experience and remediation in order to imagine a world where the poor were cared for and where both rich and poor could eat at the same table together. Because of this, the leaders within early Roman Christianity like Justin Martyr developed a process of discipleship by forming new kinds of habits that would move them to true freedom. "Justin sees the Roman's life as a habitus of *un-freedom* characterized by addictive practices . . ."[19] These practices were

---

18. Kreider, *The Patient Ferment of the Early Church*, 144.
19. Ibid., 143. Kreider notes four primary areas: sexual ethics, the occult, wealth and possessions, and violence and xenophobia. "Christians, Justin claims, have been liberated from the old habitus in order to enter a new habitus, a new

difficult to unlearn—just as they are today. But it was this regular connection of belief with practice that enabled the formation of a new kind of family-like community that was shaped by the kind of habits that were attractive and unfamiliar to outsiders.

In those days, outsiders didn't often experience the Christian witness through Christian worship. Worship gatherings were mostly private affairs. They experienced Christian habits by experiencing Christians in their daily life. The early church didn't grow in numbers because of evangelical preaching or seeker sensitivity—Christianity was illegal in Rome until the 300s. The faith grew because Christians lived compelling lives alongside the lives of non-Christians. Non-Christians asked questions about why their Christian friends lived the way they did. These questions sometimes led to an opportunity for their Christian friends to sponsor them for the catechumenate, what amounted to a three-year formation process for Christian beliefs and habits. The friend would have served as a sponsor and spiritual companion for the journey. During the process, new believers were taught the story of Scripture with particular attention to the stories of Jesus. They learned to pray and to expect the miraculous. Their bodies were formed as they learned to

---

normal. . . . Christians have renounced their old habitus and entered an alternative, life-giving habitus in each of the four areas: in sex, continence; in place of magic, dedication to God; in wealth, 'bringing what we have into a common fund and sharing with everyone in need'; in violence and xenophobia, 'living together and praying for our enemies, and trying to persuade those who unjustly hate us.'"

make the sign of the cross. They cared for the poor and provided hospitality to all. These new Christians made room for the weak and the stranger—a radical act. The process enacted through the catechumenate was symbolic of Israel's journey through the desert, across the river, and into the promised land. For the new Christian, the practice of baptism was a symbolic journey across the Jordan River. New Christians were baptized naked—a sign of vulnerability and rebirth—into a new family. This new family harkened back to the original human state and the original family. The newly baptized were dressed in a robe and entered the worship gathering where they received the bread and cup of Eucharist for the very first time.[20]

While the days of the three-year catechumenate are long gone, today we need a new—and conscious—appraisal for the formation of Christian habits. The household nature of the early church inspires us to consider how we might form the habits necessary to follow Jesus. In the next chapter, we'll take a look at a way of Christian worship that encourages the active participation of the whole group as a way of forming faithful Christians today.

---

20. Even today the Catholic Rite for the Initiation of Adults is based on this earlier catechumenal process culminating in baptism during the Easter Vigil.

Questions for Reflection

- This chapter describes hospitality as different from entertaining. Are you willing to invite someone to your home for a visit even when you're in the middle of cooking or folding laundry? If not, why?
- What do you remember about your first conversation about Jesus? Where were you and who were you with?
- What is the liturgy of your home? What simple gestures and acts shape your everyday life? How might you develop these gestures into spiritual practices?
- The life of discipleship is "as you go." How might you usher discipleship into the everyday moments?

What then shall we say, brothers and sisters? When you come together, each of you has a hymn, or a word of instruction, a revelation, a tongue or an interpretation. Everything must be done so that the church may be built up.

—1 Corinthians 14:26

CHAPTER

FOUR

The Priest at Your Elbow: Worship in the Family Community

In his book *The Patient Ferment of the Early Church,* missionary and Mennonite scholar Alan Kreider argued that the early church grew because the early Christians developed a pattern of life that was distinct from the typical patterns of the day. Those who sought a place in the Christian community went through a process of unlearning, learning, and relearning. Over time, they gave up their old patterns of life, replacing them with practices reflective of their new identity. Kreider comes from a Christian experience that is very much at home with the idea that faith begins at *home.* His view of early Christian history is a bit tidy for some, but as a Mennonite missionary his perspective is an invaluable resource for how we consciously practice the Christian faith.[1]

1. Alan Kreider (1941–2017) was a professor at Anabaptist Mennonite Biblical Seminary. He and his wife, Eleanor, served as missionaries in England for nearly twenty-five years.

While the three-year process of catechesis was important for early Christian practice, it was the worship of the early church that sustained Christian identity. Worship is the practice of *ascribing worth* to the one holy and undivided Trinity. It was and is the heart of Christian practice and Christian mission today. In worship, we learn the kind of gestures that shape our lives. In early Christianity, "God, known to them through Jesus Christ—whose words and ways were often surprising—was unconventional and was making *them* unconventional. Christ's sayings functioned not only as material to teach in their worship but also as organizing principles that guided their acts and gestures in worship."[2]

I spoke earlier of the baptismal font at the entrance of the Anglican church where we dipped our fingers and made the sign of the cross. Every time we came and went, the little droplets of water on our forehead served as a remembrance of our own baptism. When the liturgy of worship began, we stood. We bowed reverently as a team of mostly children and teenagers carried the cross and candles down the aisle. We said some of the same words every week. We knelt for a time of confession every week. We celebrated Communion every week.

While the repetition of these words and acts of devotion is often met with suspicion, for me there was something beautifully habit-forming and even identity-shaping about this rhythm. While the various streams

---

2. Alan Kreider, *The Patient Ferment of the Early Church: The Improbable Rise of Christianity in the Roman Empire* (Grand Rapids: Baker Academic, 2016), 186.

of the Christian tradition have fascinated me from an early age, the rhythm of the liturgy didn't begin to shape my practice until I became an adult. Of course, it should be said that liturgy should come from the heart. Otherwise it can become rote, boring, and just plain awful. I know people who grew up Anglican, Catholic, or Orthodox who have found a more robust faith in non-denominational, Baptist, and other free church traditions and I know plenty of people for whom the reverse is true. In my own life, I need both. I appreciate the exuberance and simplicity of my Baptist roots and the grounding of the ancient tradition. I've noticed that the same is true in the lives of our friends.

One evening in the middle of a pleasant conversation around the dinner table, a friend's young son took a water cracker from his plate, stood upon his chair, held the cracker above his head, broke it in two, and exclaimed: "The feast!"

Then he got down from his chair and gave a piece of cracker to everyone gathered around the table.

My friend's young son was simply mirroring what he'd witnessed week after week during worship. My friends were raised in an evangelical charismatic tradition but now regularly worshiped in an Anglican church. Every week, my friend's son watched as the priest stood at the table and recited the words: "Christ, our Passover, has been sacrificed for us" (see 1 Corinthians 5:7).

Then, every week, the priest would lift the bread—which looks a lot like a big cracker—and snap it.

Every week when the people in the congregation hear the snap, they exclaim: "Therefore, let us keep the feast!"

From the earliest days of the church, worship has centered around a feast. During the Roman Empire, the feasting was held over several hours often on a Saturday or Sunday evening. Everyone brought food and a word to share. We learn in 1 Corinthians what Paul thought about the ones who didn't do a very good job of sharing: "I do not commend you, because when you come together it is not for the better but for the worse" (11:17 NRSV).

As we've said, Christianity was illegal in those days. Being part of the church was risky. As Christianity became more accepted, restrictions loosened. Gatherings became public. The church grew. As it did, the patterns of worship became more efficient. Gone were the days where everyone shared a hymn, a word, or an interpretation. There were more people and less sharing. Participation was mostly limited to gestures—kneeling, bowing, and making the sign of the cross. Then there were the spoken responses—like the one demonstrated by my friend's son that night around the dinner table. Over time, the church moved from being small-scale and family-centered to large-scale and professionally led.

The Fresh Expressions movement has long given priority to fostering the connection between inherited forms of church—like the one with the big choir or the baptismal font at the entryway—and new forms of church that can happen in our living room or around our kitchen table. We call this the *mixed economy* (where there is plenty of room for different styles and rhythms of church in the same denominational family) or the *blended ecology* (where one particular church is able to express itself in different ways). Here, a symbiotic relationship exists between old and new so there is increased opportunity for greater levels of participation and different points of entry. Too often, the public perception of church is rooted in the larger scale or more formalized modes of operation.

Mixed Economy of Church—Churches of different rhythms and styles are given permission by the leadership to thrive within the same network or denomination. In this way, different kinds of churches can reach different types of people.

Blended Ecology of Church—The local congregation expresses itself in both *inherited* and *fresh* expressions of church. Fresh expressions of church are Christian communities for people who are not being reached by the inherited church. Think of inherited churches as you do inherited resources or modes of operating. You can inherit personality traits from your family the same as you can inherit an heirloom. The ways of being church we inherit are both formal and traditional or informal and contemporary in style. In fact, a fresh expression of church could be a smaller more liturgical form of a large informal church. Fresh expressions of church meet in all sorts of settings: homes, parks, and public places. Some meet weekly, others meet monthly. Some meet on Sundays, others meet at different times during the week.

For example, many people today think about church the way they do about large, impersonal agricultural corporations. While there is a sizable segment of the population that appreciates those large-scale operations, there is a growing segment of society that wants to buy local. They want to know the name of the farmer and where their food comes from. Some are even learning how to farm for themselves. The same is true for church.

When Carey and I were called to the work of creating a fresh expression of church out of a declining denominationally connected college ministry, we realized that there were plenty of larger-scale inherited forms of church around. So we set our sights on smaller, lighter-weight ways of being church instead. These forms of church grew out of our life as a couple. Because Carey and I were a little family and because many in the college and young-adult demographic were looking for family-like community more than they were looking for church, we gave it an honest start. The way wasn't clear. Tilling the soil was difficult. Changing the defaults from programmed ways of doing ministry to patterns that grew naturally out of our life together made for more restless nights than I can count. There weren't many examples of how to create new, non-programmatic ways of doing ministry while remaining connected to a historic denominational institution, so the temptation to give up altogether or to default to the commercial model was especially strong. But it became clear that we couldn't do one or the other. We had to somehow be a denominationally connected college campus ministry even as we were becoming church for people who didn't know that church was what they were looking for.

When Maddie was a freshman, she, like so many of her friends, assumed that it was impossible to be a Christian in college. College was supposed to be a break from the rigors of the spiritual life. Christianity was something to reconsider later—after having "my time" or "finding myself." After a difficult semester of loneliness and fatigue in a "dark place filled with glimmers of temporary happiness," Maddie found her way to our community and a new sense of peace. As she began the process of putting her faith back together, I asked her to sum up our community in one sentence.

"That's easy," she said. "We're church for a generation that doesn't know that *church* is what they're looking for."

In our community, we like to differentiate between annual gardening and perennial gardening. Most ministry programming is like annual gardening. Annual plants—pansies, begonias, and impatiens, for example—add a splash of color to the garden. By the end of the season these plants die. So, the gardener digs them up and plants something else. But perennial plants—like daisies, salvia, and sage—*multiply*. It takes up to three years to get the same splash of color that you get with an annual, but perennial roots grow deeper, and their flowers grow back year after year. When the good gardener digs up a perennial, it's not because it's dead, it's because it's multiplied and needs to be replanted someplace else.

I like gardening. But I don't have the time or the space to create bigger flower beds in my own yard. Besides, many of my plants were given to me. So, when my plants multiply, I try to give them away too.

As we'll see later, the economics of gift is what drives this way of thinking. Seeing one another as gift is at the heart of what it means to be family and it's at the heart of what it means to be the church. In the larger scale, inherited church way of thinking, there aren't always the mental models or the physical space necessary to expand. So we keep tending the soil we've been given, often with limited results. But if we can reorient our lives around the families that make up the church—taking some of the inheritance from the one place and planting it someplace else—there's always room to grow. We can't give what we don't have, but when we are willing and able to give ourselves away, those around us learn to give themselves away too. In the big family of God, everyone participates, and everyone grows because everyone learns to give themselves away. As we learn the practice of self-giving, the little churches multiply life just like the plants in the perennial garden and the big church is strengthened in the process.

I've described how the liturgy of the church influences the everyday practices at home. In this way we see how the inheritance of the big church gives life to the little church just like parents give life to children and children give life back to their parents. It isn't either big *or* small but is both big *and* small. It's gathered and scattered. It's both/and/also as the mission of God flows through the people of God.[3]

---

3. I'm grateful for Leonard Sweet's and Michael Beck's thinking around the both/and/also nature of church from everywhere.

When we organize the big church around the family-community of the little church we give space for everyone to participate. When we do, we see worship, community, and mission happening before us in real time. We also see how the little church is connected to the greater whole. In the family-community of radical kinship, the worship gathering acts as a point of confluence between the adoration of God, growth in God, and mission with God.

In our community, we gather for worship in several ways each week, but the pattern that has shaped us most profoundly is the pattern of *community-family evangelism* gleaned from our friend Don Renzo Bonetti. For Bonetti, this pattern of worship is where the concept of domestic church gains the most traction. Like the habits formed in the early church, this pattern of worship is designed to give all who gather what Bonetti calls "an appointed time with Jesus." Bonetti wants those participating to consciously acknowledge that it is Jesus who convenes the gathering of the church, not us. This helps develop patterns of behavior like Jesus, echoing the heart of Jesus. The pattern of worship is filled with questions and moments that trigger an emotional response rather than a purely intellectual one. By speaking from the heart, we better learn to listen for the voice of Jesus. Listening shapes a new kind of identity rooted in kinship with God.

The pattern of worship is simple, but it only works when the leaders see it as an outgrowth of their life

---

See their book *Contextual Intelligence: Unlocking the Ancient Secret to Mission on the Front Lines* (Ovieto, FL: HigherLife, 2020).

with Jesus. Again, we can't give what we don't have. The worship of the church can't be viewed as another duty, obligation, or item on the calendar. It's a time and place where the visibility of God is multiplied and shows how the love of God can be actualized in a person's life and replicated in the life of another.

We've adapted Bonetti's pattern over the years, making slight adjustments depending on the day or the season of the year. This pattern is portable and participatory, giving an opportunity for the adoration of God, growth of the disciple, and outward-facing mission within the context of family-like community.

Bonetti designed the format as a practical way to model the little church as a complement to the big church. He intends these small gatherings of six to fifteen people to be led by Jesus. They are facilitated by a married couple in a home as a way of making the reality of Jesus present in family life. Matrimony is not the point, but in this context the married couple serves as a symbol of the interpersonal communion of God.

While we've also adapted the practice with groups of up to thirty to forty people, smaller communities better cultivate attitudes of prayerful listening. Again, this gathering is not meant to be one more item on the calendar. It is a holy and set-apart time. These gatherings are *close* but not *closed*. They are open to the surrounding community, including people from the local church community as well as friends and neighbors who may have little or no current connection to the Christian faith. The hope is for these gatherings to grow and multiply throughout neighborhoods with oversight by some sort of central connection with a local church, denomination, or church network. I will provide an outline for the gathering.

The Gathering

Thanksgiving

The pattern of worship begins with a psalm, corporate singing (or sometimes listening to a song), followed by a time of thanksgiving where those in the group have the opportunity say what they are thankful for in a way that is simple and direct. Expressing gratitude opens up a pathway to God and is often an early step in cultivating a person's prayer life. This act of thanksgiving often helps grow the confidence of people who are uncomfortable speaking or praying out loud in a group. Often, it's good for the facilitator to ask those who typically speak first to hold off on sharing in order to allow space for those who aren't as comfortable sharing.

We ask: "What are you thankful for this week?" Those who respond say: "I'm thankful for ________." or "Thank you, God, for ________." Sometimes those in the group affirm the thanksgiving by saying, "Thank you, Lord." This develops a reflexive habit in the group that makes people more aware of gratitude in everyday life. Ryan, one of the guys in our little church, often reminds us that we should live thankful lives. He says that "sharing our thanksgivings at church on Sunday helps us do the same over lunch with a friend on a Tuesday."

Personal Sharing

At each gathering, we ask two questions that help reposition our hearts and minds to continue the journey of looking for Jesus in the midst of everyday life:

"What has Jesus done for you?"

"How has Jesus loved the world through you?"

The wording of these two questions is tailored to the context of the group in ways that nurture a posture of giving and receiving. Sharing what Jesus has done for us is a way of describing how we *receive* love. Sharing how Jesus loves the world through us is a way of *giving* love. Most of us are better at one or the other.

Sometimes we find it helpful to phrase the questions in a different way, particularly for those who have not thought about Jesus in such a personal way before:

"How have you been blessed this week?"

"How have you been a blessing to others?"

The stories from these times of sharing help bolster the faith of the whole group. For example, Chris, John, and Matthew share a house together. One night while they were out at a restaurant, Chris saw a man sitting alone. Chris felt led to pay the man's check. One week, Chris shared this example as a way that Jesus loved the world through him. After the check was paid, the man—Pete—introduced himself to the young men and expressed his gratitude for the gesture. He told them he owned a barbershop and offered them haircuts. "This," Chris said, "is what Jesus did for me." The following day, Chris and his housemate John went to the barbershop and got haircuts. They learned that Pete and his coworkers are Christians. They didn't just go for one haircut. Pete has become their barber. He and the other guys at the shop, along with most of the other customers, are African American. Chris and John are Caucasian. Several of Chris and John's friends have started going to Pete for haircuts too. My best guess is that there is probably more going on in this barbershop to increase deeper relationships in our city than could ever be organized in a more formal way—all because of Chris's commitment to being an agent of Jesus' self-giving love.

A few years ago, we printed the words "Start Dreaming Again" on some high-quality T-shirts. There's no formal mention of our organization on the shirts. Just those three words. Often the testimonies provoked by the two questions stem from encounters people have while wearing one of these shirts. Gordon plays sax in a band, and while his bandmates are intrigued by Gordon's faith, they are mostly indifferent to it. Gordon wore his "Start Dreaming Again" shirt to rehearsal one night and those three words sparked a discussion among his bandmates about the importance of not giving up on their dreams. The conversation provided an opening for Gordon to share how his faith shapes his dreams and the kind of dreams we read about in Scripture—when swords are made into ploughshares and when the lion lies down with the lamb.

Every week, the family-like community convened by our little church shares these kinds of stories about how the love of Jesus breaks into the everyday. J. R. Briggs, who planted the Renew Community in Landsdale, Pennsylvania, likes to say that we should live as missionaries cleverly disguised as good neighbors. While that statement could seem disingenuous, I think it's fair to say that if we consciously practice being good neighbors, over time, we will also become known by our neighbors, resulting in a change in our life and maybe even their life too. These times of personal sharing help us build our confidence and help us step out in faith as we learn to be good neighbors who become known by our neighbors as well.

Hearing and Responding to Scripture

Next, we hear and respond to a passage of Scripture together. Carey and I, along with our other leaders, read and meditate upon the daily lectionary texts.[4] Then we meet on Zoom to determine which passage seems best for the week. If there are challenging words or theological concepts in the text, we discuss this with the other leaders beforehand. The ancient practice of *Lectio Divina* guides our hearing and response to the Scripture reading. The process of Lectio Divina causes us to slow down to really hear and consider the words as they are read.

During our time of worship, we read the selected passage of Scripture four times. It works well to use the same translation of Scripture, but in our community, we ask two men and two women to read out loud from whatever translation they wish. At the first reading, we ask the group to notice a word or phrase that grabs their attention. Then we wait. At the second reading, we ask

4. For a helpful lectionary resource, see www.workingpreacher.org.

what that word or phrase might mean for them. Then we wait again. At the third reading, we ask what that word or phrase might mean for us. Then we take turns sharing the words and phrases. I love the art and craft of preaching—and have spent many an hour preparing carefully researched sermon notes and manuscripts—but I must say that, week after week, the response to the Scripture in this little church gathering is as powerful as any sermon I could preach. It also gives voice to people who didn't know they, too, could expound upon the Scriptures in a way that ministers to people and changes lives.

One Sunday while reading Matthew 25, Gordon was struck by the phrase, *"I was in prison and you visited me"* (v. 36 NRSV, italics added). Gordon works in law enforcement and confessed that he often thinks more about putting people in prison rather than visiting them there. Natalie was struck by the phrase: *"but when was it that we saw . . . ?"* (vv. 37–39, paraphrased) because she said it implies that those who do good are so consistent at it that it becomes second nature. They aren't even aware of their actions.

Our friend Becca has several years of experience in ministry leadership, but it was only after becoming part of our little family-community that she was introduced to reading the Scriptures in this way. She was skeptical at first, but over a period of months, this quiet, reflective pattern helped her slow down and listen. Prior to this, the Scriptures were something she studied, prepared, and dissected. She taught Scripture. Those in her various ministry groups responded to the teaching she prepared. Never before had she thought to let the Scriptures speak to the group. Now Becca has incorporated patterns of listening into her daily devotions and in her ministry with others. Listening is making her a more thoughtful and attentive leader.

Lectio Divina doesn't take much time to prepare. It just requires a prepared person with the skill and ability to facilitate conversation and sharing from the whole group. Again, this means that the leader suggests that the first person to speak the previous week is not the first person to speak the next week. Sometimes there are long pauses between one person's sharing and the sharing of another. That's okay. The moments of quiet enable participants to collect their thoughts before they offer their own response to the Word. These moments cause us to slow down so that we can really encounter Jesus.

Announcements

At each gathering, the facilitator asks the group if there are any announcements related to the local church, neighborhood, or community. While this can often be a time of dead air in most worship services, for us this is a time of fresh air as we're reminded of our connections to something larger than ourselves or our little gathering.

Prayer for Those Outside the Group

After the announcements, we pray for needs outside the group. My colleague Chris Morton, who's experimented with this pattern of worship in his community in Austin, Texas, says that "this goes beyond 'sick friends and relatives,' although that's definitely part of it!" Together the group prays out loud for the needs of specific friends, neighbors, coworkers, or family members who are not in the group. We pray for them by name as this helps orient the group to real needs of real people beyond the group. We also use this time to pray for needs in our community, our nation, and our world.

Prayer for Someone in the Group

Next, we pray for individual persons in the group. Rather than asking which person in the group wants to receive prayer, we often ask whether or not anyone in the group has someone here on their mind for prayer. I'm never sure how this works, but almost always two people in the group have the same person in mind. If this person is willing to receive prayer, we create space for silence where the group can listen to God on their behalf. Then we share what we hear. (For example: we ask if God gives you a word, a picture, a scripture, or even a cartoon character for the person, they should feel free to share it with a caveat: it might be from God . . . or it might be because they ate too much pizza the night before!). We approach this and all times of sharing humbly and reverently. We don't know if these words are "directly from God for others," but we believe they could be.

When we allow space to hear from God on behalf of another person, we continue building the spiritual confidence of those gathered in the group (and even those outside as the stories are shared). It is not uncommon for someone to tell their friends what happened to them during prayer last week at house church or for an answered prayer to become the subject of the time of personal sharing the next time we meet. After the silence and the sharing, we ask if the person has any other specific needs or requests. Often their requests have already been accounted for simply because we held space to listen to this person. We also make it our practice to record this portion as a gift and a helpful reminder for the person receiving prayer.

Once we were praying for Tiffany—someone in the group who didn't consider herself a Christian. During the time of silence, two different people in the group got the same word for her. The word was *sandman*. As in "Mr. Sandman . . . bring me a dream." Tiffany went on to explain that she'd been having trouble sleeping. No one else knew this. So, we prayed that Tiffany would sleep through the night.

On another occasion, two people got the word *roadrunner* while we were praying for our friend Jill. It seemed almost ridiculous until Michael, one of the guys in our group, did a quick word search on his phone for the symbolic meaning of the roadrunner only to discover that it's a sign of Epiphany, healing, or the completion of a phase or a goal in life. The word resonated with Jill. She had, in fact, been through a lot of healing and had just completed work on a new business plan. We don't over-analyze these moments. We don't dwell on whether or not a word search on the Internet is the best theological tool for use during prayer. We simply rejoice when a word meets someone where they are, and we give thanks that God is at work in the midst of our life together.

The Lord's Prayer

We close the time by saying the Lord's Prayer aloud. Bonetti challenges his groups to pray in an outward-facing circle as a sign that our mission of love is for the world.

> Our Father, who art in heaven,
> hallowed be thy Name,
> thy kingdom come,
> thy will be done,
> on earth as it is in heaven.
> Give us this day our daily bread.
> And forgive us our trespasses,
> as we forgive those
> who trespass against us.
> And lead us not into temptation,
> but deliver us from evil.
> For thine is the kingdom,
> and the power, and the glory,
> for ever and ever. Amen.[5]

When the Family-Community Birthed in the "Little Church" Has the Option of Becoming "Fully Church"—A Word about the Fresh Expressions Journey

This process of participatory worship in the family-community is a powerful and practical outworking of the little church. In many cases, this pattern of worship

5. *Book of Common Prayer* (New York: Oxford University Press, 1979), 364.

is intended as a complement to the gathering of the big church on Sunday. In other cases, it provides a road map for a way of planting a distributed form of church through a network of house churches. When the global pandemic made large worship gatherings impossible, this format sustained, matured, and grew our faith community. In everything, context matters. What works in one place will not work in every place. We'd spent nearly a decade reimagining a denominationally supported college campus ministry along the Fresh Expressions journey in hopes of it someday becoming more fully church.

Again, what we call "fresh expressions of church" are initiatives and experiments that help form church among those who are not yet reached by any church. The fresh expressions journey starts by *listening to the community.* As we listen, we discover a population with specific needs. Whereas many expressions of church start with a worship service, this process of listening leads to what we call *loving-service.* How do we best meet the needs of the population to which we are called? Over time, a shared *community is built* among a few people who are willing to explore the life of Christian discipleship. Then a *form of church* begins to more clearly develop. This process is not even as linear as it sounds (which isn't very!). There are all sorts of variables in every context. Because every Christian family is already a little church, our question becomes about how families might expand their reach to include others who may be far from God's love in a process of becoming a fresh expression of church together.

As we listened within our own community, we met lots of young people who were in college, but we also met many who weren't. They needed a supportive community but didn't know where to look. Many of the students and young adults had little or no connection to church. Those who did have church experience were often looking for a deeper experience of faith. Because our community had become their primary way of experiencing the depth of Christian community, they had started referring to our community as "church." In the months leading up to the pandemic, we had been taking the steps necessary to more fully consider this reality. Various other contextual factors played a role in our story. Several of our young people started experimenting with intentional living in shared houses. As I shared earlier, a house across the street from where some of them lived came up for sale and Carey and I moved there to be in closer proximity to them. A few months later another group of young people moved into a house two blocks away. The close proximity deepened our experience of family-like community. At the start of the COVID-19 pandemic, our close proximity to one another became a lifeline. We began convening our larger community for discipleship and leadership training online, but since we could meet in groups of up to ten in person, we began experimenting with the liturgy of family-community evangelism. The initial group met on our front porch. Once some of the pandemic restrictions loosened, we added to our number, meeting outside whenever possible.

Over the next nine months, our community began the process of formally becoming a network of house churches, open to all, but with a mission focus on the college and young adult population. I am ordained to ministry within the Baptist tradition and chiefly view my role as an equipper of the saints for the work of ministry. I take seriously a still unexplored insight of the great reformer Martin Luther: the "priest at every elbow." This means that we are "priests to each other," the "priesthood of every believer."[6] This means that I am continuously giving myself, my skills, and my leadership away to others so that the ministry will thrive and flourish. I didn't come to this conclusion easily, but I have found great freedom in learning to multiply leadership. It's required that I lose control without sacrificing oversight. Prior to the coronavirus pandemic, our ministry was at capacity. For the ministry to grow—and for our leaders not to burn out—we had to multiply others to carry the work.[7] We are attentive to doing things in order according to our context and tradition. I am acutely aware of cell church and other ministry models that lean into strategies for multiplication without fully considering the natural growth and development of people into healthy leaders. It's good to have a strategy for multiplication, but I want to be clear that focusing on multiplication at the expense of healthy family-community is not the goal. Communion with God and fruitfulness in life is the goal. Lots of married couples have an *idea* of how many children they would like to

---

6. Carlyle Marney, *Priests to Each Other* (Nashville: Abingdon, 1974), xi.

7. It is worth noting that I am in the unique position of working in the ministry of Fresh Expressions and while there is a natural point of intersection in the local ministry, I do not at this point receive compensation for the building of the local body of believers. There are trade-offs to this co-vocational model, of course, but it makes multiplication of leaders all the more necessary.

have, for example, but it doesn't always work out that way. In chapter 6 we'll look at this concept of ministry strategy and the will through the lens of eros and agape love.

In our context of multiplication, we are creating a process to commission our household leaders to the work of local ministry, and we are training them to facilitate the family-community evangelism process along with the celebration of Communion and baptism. Our Sunday community gatherings are now distributed and hosted in several homes, each following a pattern similar to what we've outlined. These home-based churches meet weekly, and in a larger big church gathering once a month. Again, this is all contextual. What works in some places and in some church contexts will need to be modified in others depending on the denomination, structure, and tradition.

In our context, Carey and I convene all of the home-gathering leaders weekly in person or online. During this weekly meeting, we discuss any pastoral care needs they or their group may have along with discerning together which scripture passage we will use for the week. Our relationships with the leaders are mutual and reciprocal. We discern the needs of the community together. Leaders agree to follow a set of covenant principles outlined in our community way of life to make sure everyone is on the same page and to ensure mutual accountability, relationship, and shared mission.

The Pattern of Family-Community Evangelism

Family-community evangelism is a pattern of participatory worship usually led by couples or families in a home as a way to demonstrate the little church as part of a bigger congregation or church network. Reflect upon the following and how it might be helpful in your setting:

Thanksgiving

What are you thankful for?

Personal Sharing

What has Jesus done for you?

How has Jesus loved the world through you?

Hearing and Responding to Scripture[8]

Listen

Begin with a few moments of quiet or a prayer.

Facilitator: "During the first reading, listen for a specific word or phrase that grabs your attention."

Have one person read the passage aloud and allow for a time of quiet reflection.

---

8. My colleague Chris Morton provided this helpful adaptation of *Lectio Divina*, an ancient practice of scripture reading dating from the third century. As we hear the scripture read, we enter the presence of Jesus and our words of reflection on the reading become a sacrament—an outward sign of the inner grace given by Jesus.

Meditate

Facilitator: "During the second reading, meditate on that word or phrase. Ask God what it means."

Have a person read the passage aloud a second time and allow for a time of quiet reflection.

Share

Facilitator: "During the third reading, meditate on what this word might be saying to you or to the group."

Have a person read the passage aloud a third time. After a time of quiet reflection, allow for a time of sharing of any relevant words from the scripture that was read.

Savor

Facilitator: "During the fourth reading, let go of words and allow the Word to rest upon you." This is a time of contemplation with God in the body—your holy temple.

Have a person read the passage aloud a fourth time.

Community Announcements

Prayer

Pray for the needs outside the group.

Initiate a listening prayer for one person inside the group. (Record the prayer time and give it as a gift!)

The Lord's Prayer

This can be prayed in an outward-facing circle to symbolize our life given for the world.

If an unbeliever invites you to a meal and you are disposed to go, eat whatever is set before you without raising any question on the ground of conscience.

—1 Corinthians 10:27 (NRSV)

CHAPTER

FIVE

A Table Bigger than Your House: When to Be a Guest and Not a Host

When Dave and Maria were newlyweds, they started making a pot of soup and a loaf of bread on Thursday nights at their house, a little 1950's rental. Every week, they invited their friends and neighbors over to enjoy their soup and bread. Every week, for about six months, Dave and Maria sat at their kitchen table eating their soup and bread alone. But they kept at it. Every week they remained faithful and prayerful. One Thursday night, a neighbor finally came. The next week the neighbor brought a coworker. Soon their table was full. On one of those full-table nights, a friend of a friend—a young and boisterous restaurant manager—showed up with a bottle of wine. Dave and Maria didn't often drink wine. But that night they did, and the boisterous young man soon became a part of the family. By the time I met that boisterous young man, he was my landlord and the director of mercy ministries at a local church. I met Dave and Maria about fifteen years later during their daughter's freshman year in college. They lived just down the street from the university and became known to us as the pancake parents. On Saturday mornings, a rumpus of students rambled down the hill from the campus to the neighborhood below and into their home. The aromas of bacon, butter, and syrup filled the air. As the students pulled together an assortment of chairs around the big family table, their plates were piled high with piping hot pancakes. There was no catch, no bait and switch. Dave and Maria weren't out for anything but making pancakes for their daughter's friends. Dave and Maria's life is a gift, and they know how to share it with others. Between their four kids and the countless international students they've hosted in their home over the years, there's rarely a spare bed in their house. When our mutual friend Jill was looking for a supportive community around which to plan the launch of her new business, she happily moved in with Dave and Maria.

Dave and Maria will tell you that there's nothing perfect about their life. Their house is lived in. Mr. Bingley, their Golden Retriever, noses his way into nearly every conversation, and that's part of what makes their home such a wonderful place to be—and become. It's a place where the door is almost always open and where there's always a seat at the table.

There's something about a table. We eat at the table, talk at the table, and work at the table. We draw pictures, arrange puzzles, and play games around the table. Once we lived in a house where the washer and dryer were tucked inside a closet under the stairs in the dining room next to the table. So, at that house, we folded our laundry at the table too.

Early Christian gatherings happened almost exclusively around the table. Before Jesus' death, his disciples gathered around the table to celebrate the Passover. After his resurrection, his followers recognized him in the breaking of the bread (Luke 24:28–32). The early Christians "broke bread in their homes" (Acts 2:46). We said earlier that Christian gatherings were dinner parties held over several hours on a Saturday or Sunday night. These parties were modeled on the custom of the Roman supper clubs where members paid the dues required for entry so they could celebrate certain ways of life and certain gods. These supper clubs met according to social class. Christian supper clubs, on the other hand, were a living witness of radical kinship. Christian gatherings made space at the table for members of every social and economic class. Some of the early Christians were accustomed to certain table manners; others were accustomed to no particular manners at all.

The general pattern of these early gatherings began with the breaking of the bread—*take, eat, this is my body given for you*—followed by a meal. After supper they took the cup of wine—*drink this, all of you*—as a sign of Christ's blood shed for the forgiveness of sins (see Matthew 26:26–27). After the main meal, the Christian community retired to another room of the house or apartment block where they were served smaller plates of fruit and dessert. At this point, they entered into a time of participatory worship where everyone brought a word or testimony to share. In the second century, some of these Christian gatherings began meeting before daylight on Sunday morning. Since Sunday was a workday for many (and it still is) the gathering had to be shorter and more scripted. The feast was celebrated but the food was tokenized. There was less emphasis on a shared community and more power placed in the hands of a few.[1] Over time, the worship gathering put greater emphasis on the individual rather than the communal encounter with Jesus. The Eucharist became a reminder of the banquet feast and a vehicle for understanding and tending the presence of Christ.

For centuries, Christ's presence in worship has been associated with the Eucharistic feast. Over time, the table became a kind of thin place. It was (and is) a beautiful picture enjoyed by many Christians today, but this kind of table fellowship often has little associated memory with or connection to the fellowship once experienced in the homes of those early believers. By the Reformation, the practice of the Eucharist, Lord's Supper, or Holy Communion became so contested that many later generations of Christians (short of the recovery of the love feast by the Moravians in the 1720s)[2] either overlooked

---

1. See Alan Kreider, *The Patient Ferment of the Early Church: The Improbable Rise of Christianity in the Roman Empire* (Grand Rapids: Baker Academic, 2016), 186–92.

2. The early Methodists adopted this practice in the 1740s from the Moravians as a form of table fellowship separate from Holy Communion. In both traditions, only ordained clergy can preside at Communion, but the love feast can be celebrated at any time.

it or didn't engage in the regular practice of the banquet or the Eucharist hardly at all. Generations of Christians never had the opportunity to develop the habits or the spiritual imagination arising from the Eucharistic feast. Fast-forward to our day of fast pace and fast food, and we're in desperate need of recovering the power of the table.

I recall a Catholic bishop telling me once that he thought there were plenty of Catholic Christians—some who take the Eucharist every day—who risk approaching the Lord's Table as a party of one with little thought of the grander view of the great big family table. Even though the Eucharist has most often been separated from the original context, it remains an enduring demonstration of the ongoing, self-giving love of Jesus the bridegroom for his bride—the church. One day all who are part of the bride will share in the marriage supper of the Lamb. Until that day, the table plays a role in forming and shaping us as a people of the way—on the way. Bonetti suggests that "evangelization and mission are intimately connected to the Eucharist, because Eucharist is Jesus going to meet his people. When we fail to engage in this going, we nullify his mission and cancel the purpose of Jesus' donation. Too often, we eat the Eucharist, give thanks for it, and feel better—but lack the element of mission and evangelization."[3]

In his book *Faithful Presence: Seven Disciplines That Shape the Church for Mission,* David Fitch argues for a

---

3. Renzo Bonetti, *Signs of Love: Christian Liturgy in the Everyday Life of the Family,* trans. Alessandro Sona and Brent Orrell (Franklin, TN: Seedbed, 2017), 47.

recovery of the table for the sake of mission. Fitch hails from the stream of North American evangelicalism that has sometimes overlooked the table and he's become an influential leader in helping drive the practice of the Lord's Table back to the center of the church's worship. From this place, he shows how the worship of the church flows into the rest of life. He presents the practice of the table in three ways: the table in the close circle, the table in the dotted circle, and the table in the half circle.

The Table in the Close Circle, Dotted Circle, and Half Circle

The close circle represents the fellowship of believers gathered around the presence of Jesus. In the close circle, Jesus is at the center as the host and those in the circle are the guests. In this case, "there is a social closeness that is supernatural."[4] Fitch is careful to call this circle *close* but not *closed*. In the close circle, Christians are committed to discerning their place in community under the direction of Jesus, who doesn't exclude anyone willing to submit to his rule and reign. In Fitch's view, the close circle includes the celebration of the Eucharistic feast at every meeting. The congregation where he serves places the Lord's Table at the center of their worship space. Week after week, the presence of Christ in the close (but not closed) circle

4. David Fitch, *Faithful Presence: Seven Disciplines That Shape the Church for Mission* (Downers Grove, IL: InterVarsity Press 2016), 40.

prepares and propels the fellowship to welcome the presence of Christ everywhere.

The Lord's Table of the close circle extends into the neighborhood and around the kitchen table. Fitch depicts this table as a dotted circle where space is made for neighbors and friends to experience the presence of Jesus at the table—even when they're unaware of who Jesus is or what Jesus does. This is what our friends Dave and Maria did so well when they invited their daughter's friends for pancakes or on that night their friend Chris showed up with the bottle of wine. It's what our friend's young son meant when he shared the feast of broken cracker pieces with all those gathered around his family's table. It's what we experienced when we rolled out the burlap and placed the candlesticks down the center of our very long table. The Lord's Table gives meaning to the dotted circle around the family table. In the close circle, Jesus is the host. In the dotted circle, Jesus' followers are the hosts.

Then there is the move to the half circle—those public tables out and among the hurting and the wandering. Here, those who are most accustomed to being the hosts at home learn to become the guests in places around the public table. "In this half circle, the question is never whether Christ is here or not. Rather it is whether or not his presence will be welcomed."[5] Fitch often experiences his half circle at McDonald's. With free Wi-Fi and refills, it's a place where he can work alongside and among others he might not otherwise meet. At his home, Fitch is the host. At McDonald's, he acts as the guest. While he

5. Fitch, *Faithful Presence*, 40.

could simply be just another customer, there among the booths and the benches, amidst the aroma of hash browns and Happy Meals, Fitch has found a sense of place as a welcomed guest. His constant presence gives him opportunities to listen, encourage, and pray for those who are there. At McDonald's, Fitch has learned to welcome and tend the presence of Christ and to usher in a space of radical kinship where there is no *us* or *them*, only *us*.

Radical kinship unfolds around the table. Those in the close circle see the table as central to the Christian story through the regular sharing of the Lord's Supper. This table extends to the kitchen table in the dotted circle. From there, it extends further into the neighborhood around public tables in public spaces, enacting in various ways the dynamic story of God's incarnation that cannot be confined or contained.

If we merely tend to the presence of Christ around the table in the close circle (the upward move of our faith in this case), we miss out on tending Christ's presence in the everyday. If we pay attention only to his presence in the half circle (the outward posture of mission), we run the risk of mental, physical, and spiritual exhaustion. In this scenario, the dotted circle of the home provides a middle way between the two. The best experience of home is the inner work of the family-community that is attentive to both the upward and outward dimensions even as they ask the right questions that get at the health of the relationships at the heart of the family-community. The home serves as a little church between the big church and an outpost for mission in the world. It is a refining place, both a safe house and a greenhouse.

For too long the church has functioned without recognizing the importance of an encounter with Jesus and one another in each of the three spaces. When the church moved from the home and into buildings specifically used for church meetings, the family table moved with it. The table took on new meanings. It became more ceremonial, and the ceremony ushered in a way of worship that sustained the church in new ways through the gift of the Eucharist. But along the way the church lost the original sense of the table as a family gathering around a shared meal with greater levels of participation. What if we could extend the table of the close circle back into our homes where we could recover a shared meal and shared participation once again?

Our friends Chad and Emily have a sign hanging in their dining room that reads: "When you have more than you need, build a longer table, not a higher fence." Over the years, Chad and Emily have used their table to host Sunday suppers for their neighbors. In the early morning hours, it's not uncommon for people in Chad's running group or from Emily's fitness class to follow them back to their house, where they congregate around the kitchen island for coffee and smoothies.

The call to build a longer table is a powerful word for the church today and it is one that is deeply rooted within our Scriptures. We think here again of the kinship codes in the Torah in the welcome of women like Rahab and Ruth. There's the story of Jonah who wanted to run away from the stranger but had to face the stranger instead. Or what about Job? He wasn't part of the Israelite community at all, yet somehow he seemed to know God's will as if it were written in the very order of creation. Listening to Job means listening to a foreigner. "We learn from the book of Job that listening to those who don't share the faith of Israel may lead to greater insight into our own Scriptures."[6] All we have to do is extend the table. From the big church to the little church and out into public spaces, we gather around the table as host and as guest. When we do, we extend our hands and our hearts to envision a world where there is no *us* or *them*—only *us.*

For many years, our friends Verlon and Melodee Fosner served as pastors of a thriving middle-class church in Seattle, Washington. The church never grew in the ways they expected. After a long process of studying Jesus' practice of ministry and the history of the early church and its practice of gathering around the table, Verlon found his way into a community center just a few blocks beyond their church building and, there, a whole new place of ministry opened before him. There, he connected with people who were in desperate need of fellowship around the table. Soon he began a dinner church for people at the community center and, in a few weeks, he'd begun to witness a foretaste of the heavenly banquet as people from diverse ages and backgrounds gathered together around the table. Through his family and through the families at his church, they've been able to start ten dinner churches meeting on any given

---

6. Mark R. Glanville and Luke Glanville, *Refugee Reimagined: Biblical Kinship in Global Politics* (Downers Grove, IL: InterVarsity Press, 2021), 70.

night around tables in community centers and in other public spaces around their city. These dinner churches have effectively quadrupled the size of the church as it was when it was merely a weekly gathering in one location in the close circle. These dinner table gatherings are welcome for the stranger and a place to call home. No question or subject is off limits. Mostly they talk about life around the table. Eventually they get to limits. Inevitably in the midst of these unforced conversations they get to spiritual matters. Week after week, strangers become guests and guests become hosts. For several years now, Verlon and Melodee have been leading a movement to put dinner churches in every neighborhood in the country, using their home as a laboratory for training and equipping others on how to extend the table into every neighborhood.[7]

This is the message. The table in every home is an extension of the table in the close circle. Every marriage is an echo of the marriage supper of the Lamb. Every conversation is a treasured opportunity to declare the glory that is and the glory that one day will be.

As we look toward the day of feasting at the heavenly banquet, marriage and family-like community are not the goal. Discipleship and worship are not the goal. They are vehicles. The goal is our union with the infinite love of God.

---

7. See Verlon Fosner, *Dinner Church: Building Bridges by Breaking Bread* (Franklin, TN: Seedbed, 2017) and additional resources at DinnerChurch.com.

In his rendering of the Twenty-Third Psalm, the hymn writer Isaac Watts put it this way:

The sure provisions of my God attend me all my days;
Oh, may Thy house be my abode and all my work be praise;
There would I find a settled rest, while others go and come;
No more a stranger nor a guest, but like a child at home.[8]

Bringing church home is the call to that settled rest where we make our home within the infinitude of God's love and to recognize, in the breaking of the bread, a place of welcome that heals and restores. In Spanish and Latin American culture, the term *sobremesa* describes the unhurried, settled rest we often experience at the table after a meal. I like to think of our union with God as a permanent lingering at the table. There are no dishes that need washing. There is no place else to be, just there in God's presence. Extending the table creates opportunities for others to experience the extended presence where we are no longer strangers or hosts or guests, but fully and finally at home.

8. Isaac Watts, "My Shepherd Will Supply My Need," 1719. Public domain.

Questions for Reflection

- What have been some of your favorite times around the table? What made them special?
- Think about your experience of the table in the close circle, the dotted circle, and the half circle. How might you better acknowledge the presence of Christ in each?
- How has Jesus loved the stranger through you?
- How might your table become an extension of the Lord's Table? How does your table serve as a place of unhurried lingering and settled rest?

The earth is the LORD's and all that is in it,
the world, and those who live in it;
for he has founded it on the seas,
and established it on the rivers.

—PSALM 24:1–2 (NRSV)

CHAPTER

SIX

Becoming Human: Nothing Is Yours, Not Even the Fig Leaf

Sometimes we have to get outside of our own tradition to renew it. When we do, others may find the courage to do the same.

Every day there are thousands of little deaths and resurrections. I call them *aha* moments and *uh-oh* moments. Some of my friends call them *kairos* moments. *Kairos,* a Greek word for time, signifies a sort of spiritual breaking into the ordinary to reorder it.[1] There are moments of *aha* when we surprise ourselves with our own progress ("Aha! I'm really good at cooking or music or accounting.") or moments of *uh-oh* when we catch ourselves in the midst of our own self-deception ("Just kidding, I'm really bad at accounting and I need

1. For further reading, see Mike Breen, *Building a Discipling Culture* (Pawley's Island, SC: 3DM Publishing, 2016), 75–88.

to accept that."). The key for an *aha* or an *uh-oh* is to catch ourselves in the act and to invite God into it. God is there already, of course. We just need to acknowledge and receive it in the moment and commit to learning from it. Moments like these beg us to stop, look, and listen; observe, reflect, and discuss. With a little intention and accountability, these moments deepen our belief. What does it mean for me to be the person I was created to be? These moments bring repentance and deepen our belief. They cause a change of mind. When we live in our true humanity undergirded by the in-breaking power of God, we can't help but realize that life is a gift that we get to share with others. This is the essence of love.

Love is a powerful theme. Psychologist and Holocaust survivor Viktor Frankl wrote that "love is the highest goal to which man can aspire . . . the salvation of man is through love and in love."[2] St. John of the Cross said that in the evening of life we will be judged by love alone. St. Therese of Lisieux wrote: "To love is to give everything and to give oneself."[3] This notion of love, that our lives are a gift, is the guiding principle of what's known as the Theology of the Body, a collection of reflections developed by Polish Bishop Karol Wojtyla. After Wojtyla became Pope John Paul II, he delivered these reflections as part

---

2. Viktor Frankl, *Man's Search for Meaning* (Boston: Beacon Press, 1959), 37.
3. John Paul II, *Man and Woman He Created Them: A Theology of the Body*, from the introduction by Michael Waldstein (Boston: Pauline Books and Media, 2006), 124.

of his weekly audiences with visitors from around the world. In these reflections, he demonstrates the beauty of God's love as it is worked out in creation and in the marriage between man and woman. John Paul II is not the first word on these subjects and he won't be the last, but insofar as he depicts love, marriage, and the mystical, sacramental calling of the body, his is an important word for our time.

John Paul II roots his teaching of love and marriage within the uniqueness of every person.

The term *person* has been coined to signify that a man cannot be wholly contained within the concept of "individual member of the species," but that there is something more to him, a particular richness and perfection on the manner of his being, which can only be brought out by the use of the word *person*.[4]

Persons are rational in nature (or at least we're trying to be!). We have an inner and sensual life beyond that of plants and animals. This rational, inner life is what makes us feel loved.

While we have often been taught to think categorically about love, John Paul II's view of love and its practical outworking in the marriage relationship makes connections between unconditional love (*agape*) and romantic fulfillment (*eros*).

Agape love is the love we most often associate with God. This kind of love is patient and kind. It is not envious, boastful, or rude. It doesn't insist on its own

---

4. Karol Wojtyla, *Love and Responsibility* (Ignatius Press: San Francisco, 1993), 22.

way (1 Cor. 13:1–8). We think of eros love when our heart is racing. It's passionate love. And it also comes from God. There is a reason that Christ's crucifixion and his passion are one and the same. He endured the cross, giving all of himself unconditionally (agape), because he was zealous in his desire to redeem humanity, bringing all of us to himself (eros). The problem is that we tend to separate the two, thereby devaluing love, particularly sexual love from its truest meaning. Michael Waldstein calls this "the sexual lie, in which the language of radical gift is overlaid by the contrary language of individual autonomy and the use of persons for pleasure."[5] This has been a significant *aha* moment for me. When eros love is separated from agape love, we end up with a false picture of love that leaves us either letting our passions run wild or attempting to tame our passions without God's help (turn it off, turn it off, turn it off!) which leads to moralistic legalism. Eros, while flawed, is part of what makes us a person. It is something for which we should be thankful. When we stop attempting to outsmart our passions and allow God's unconditional love to take control of them instead, we become better able to love in the ways God intended. The same is true for *filial* relationships (love between friends) and *storge* relationships (love between parents and children). When we're able to catch ourselves in the act of being passionately tired, passionately angry, or when we have a heightened

5. John Paul II, *Man and Woman He Created Them*, from the introduction by Michael Waldstein, 126.

sense of sexual passion, I find it helpful to name it as an *aha* moment, thank God for it, and ask for God's love to break in so that our loves are infused and rightly ordered by God.

Earlier I mentioned the multiplication of Christian leaders and the tendency of some forms of ministry to focus on strategy rather than the natural and patient development of people. In this case, I find it helpful to compare agape and eros to the busy activity of Martha and the quiet contemplation of Mary in Luke 10:38–42. In this story Jesus isn't concerned with the fact that Martha is busy working, it's how she's going about her work. "Lord, tell my sister to help me!" she says. Jesus cuts right through Martha's exasperation with her sister by saying, "you are worried and distracted by many things." Action and contemplation both contain elements of all the loves, but they also contain willful and controlling patterns of behavior, causing us to prioritize duty and obligatory acts of service on the one hand—an "if I don't do it, who will?" sort of attitude. On the other hand, we can also give too much credence to overtly spiritual behavior. "Don't you know not to interrupt me when I'm spending time alone with God?" Again, the *aha* moment is coming to an awareness of both.

My attempt here will undoubtedly be seen as an over-simplification of the loves in some cases and I realize that every metaphor breaks down with overuse, but it nevertheless shows how our desire for love might come into alignment with God by becoming a holy desire rather than a willful or controlling desire.

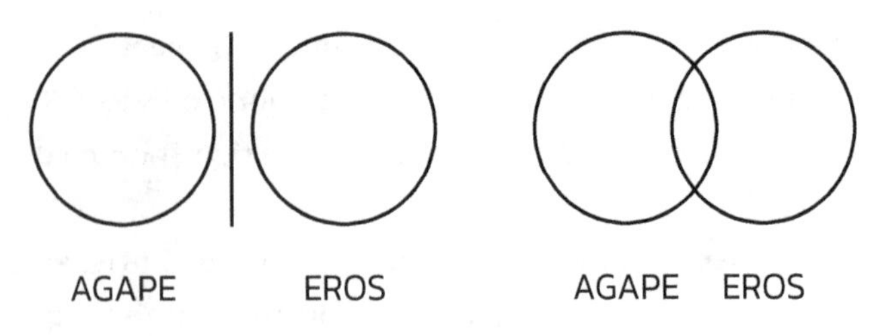

In his theology, John Paul II affirmed the goodness of sexuality as expressed in the "dynamism of the relationship between man and woman."[6] It is this dynamism that Jesus came to heal, transform, and redeem regardless of whether or not we're married.

John Paul II does not see Jesus primarily as a moralist, as teaching a high ideal of self-giving love that leaves human beings in despair about the weakness of their flesh and the failure of their attempts to measure up to ideal love. On the contrary, Jesus speaks primarily as a redeemer who overcomes sin and opens the way for real transformation and life in the Spirit. He is the redeemer of the body, who has the power to inscribe the law of love in hearts of flesh. He can demand a radical gift of self, because he has offered such a gift of himself to the human race, and his gift is effective.[7]

John Paul II shows how our human *biology* (eros) can't be interpreted apart from our *theology* (agape).

6. John Paul II, *Man and Woman He Created Them*, from the introduction by Michael Waldstein, 127.
7. Ibid.

Christopher West, a popular interpreter of John Paul II's work, argues that "Only to the degree that we know what our bodies 'say' theologically do we know who we really are and, therefore, how we are to live."[8] For John Paul II, Jesus' teaching, along with the commandments of Scripture, provide a vehicle pointing toward divine love. They are not a radical minimum standard for behavior, but a radical reordering of our approach to life. John Paul II was deeply concerned about the degradation of the human person and worried that the body was being treated as a utility when its intended purpose is to bear the image of God. If we're taught to love our neighbor as ourselves, our role is to create places (homes, schools, businesses, and churches) where this is more likely to occur.

John Paul II was born near Krakow in southern Poland. From an early age he had a fondness for outdoor adventure. As a young priest he held mass outdoors, lashing paddles together to form a cross and using upturned canoes as a makeshift holy table. In the face of Communism, he recognized the value of human freedom and preserved the faith by ministering from house to house. He believed in the power of the home and the potential of home as a domestic church. "The language of domestic church positions family as a site for the 'reproduction of the church.'"[9]

---

8. John Paul II, *Man and Woman He Created Them*, from the preface, xxix.
9. David Matzko McCarthy, *Sex and Love in the Home: A Theology of the Household* (Eugene, OR: Wifp and Stock, 2001), 114.

It was his predecessor Pope Paul VI who, during the Second Vatican Council, first coined the term "domestic church" to frame an essential component for what he believed essential for the renewal of the whole church. This term suggests that every family is a little church and part of God's plan to heal the world. Family life is foundational for understanding church as communion. God designed both to love inwardly in matters of the common life but also outwardly "through the character of the gathered body as a sign of God's presence, patterned in the way of Jesus and the life of discipleship."[10] In this way, "the family's communion and its character as domestic church . . . emphasize the family as an 'agent of transformation' . . . and an attempt to intensify the role of the household by presenting family as a contrast-society in a culture of attenuated [unnaturally thin] relations."[11]

Pope John Paul II's recognition of the inherent worth of the family stemmed from the day in which he lived. He came of age during World War II when his native Poland lost 20 percent of its population, including three million Jews—half of all the Jews murdered at the hands of Hitler's Nazi regime. He, like Dietrich Bonhoeffer, attended an underground seminary in the face of Hitler's threat. Before that, he was in an underground theatre group to keep Polish language and culture alive. He watched after the war as Poland became part of the Communist Eastern Bloc. The principles of Communism

---

10. McCarthy, *Sex and Love in the Home*, 114.
11. Ibid.

sought to dismantle the family, creating isolation, loneliness, and dependence on government. This philosophy drove people further and further apart. While religion was not outlawed outright in Communist Poland, the government made it very difficult for the church to exist. As a young priest, Wojtyla ministered from house to house, stressing the importance of marriage and family as an antidote to the threats of the day. These experiences deeply impacted his Theology of the Body.

The Three Original States

Reflecting on Genesis 1–2, John Paul II shows how our bodies inform our unique identity, preparing us for life in shared community by listing three ways that humans first experienced their life with God in creation. These original states are solitude, unity, and nakedness. In chapter 1, I discussed kinship and welcoming the stranger. Understanding these three concepts is crucial to living our radical kinship in God and how that relationship influences our attitude of welcome in every other relationship.

Original Solitude

When you think of solitude, what comes to mind? I think of sunrise on the ocean or sunset at a mountain lake. I think of my first sip of coffee before anyone else is awake. I'm an extrovert, but I'm not a morning person. Most mornings I live for stillness and solitude. But I can't survive alone. I was created for others.

The creation accounts in Genesis 1 and 2 evoke deep and symbolic meaning. While all the plants and animals are created by God, it is only people who are created in the *image* of God. What's more, because the first Adam (who, in this case, is representative of all humans) was created in God's image, Adam is given the remarkable responsibility of naming all of the animals. God enters into partnership with Adam. I can only imagine the kind of intimate solitude experienced between God and Adam in the beauty of creation. In my own moments of solitude, I glimpse it in the playfulness of the squirrels scampering up the oak tree in my yard. Or in my shock and wonder upon seeing a black bear along the trail in Shenandoah National Park. It's during times like these when I realize that it's not just solitude that I need—it's how much I also need others. Even moments of solitude with others. As much as Adam likes the playfulness—or awe—of all the animals, they're no replacement for people. We all love our pets. But they'll never relate with us in the same ways that people do. That's why God said, "It is not good for the man to be alone. I will make a helper suitable for him" (Gen. 2:18).

Original Unity

It's not good to be alone. Knowing what it means to be human is impossible without other people in our lives. Adam named the other animals, but none of these animals could name him. He needed a partner, a helper to discover his identity. The word *helper* in the Hebrew is *ezer*, which means "to save and to be strong." While humans reflect God's image through our individual rational souls, we only become aware of this reality in community with others. Nowhere is this more evident than in the creation of male and female.

"In the beginning God created the heavens and the earth" (Gen. 1:1). God separated light from darkness, the heavenly waters from the earthly waters, the sun from the moon, the land from the sea. All of creation exists in total—yet distinct—unity. As we've seen in the intersection between eros and agape, the creation of man and woman brings this even closer to our understanding. Humans are called to life together in unity but with distinction at the same time. Our personalities are different; our bodies are different. Like the sun and the moon. But there is no unity without these distinctions, only an enforced uniformity. While a certain kind of unity in distinction can be understood between any two persons or a group of people, the communion between male and female in the marriage relationship makes this plain both practically and physically. Communion in marriage holds within it the possibility of making the ordinary, extraordinary. Male and female unity bring forth human life, a deeper life with God, and a deeper life with one another. Theology of the Body makes this relationship between love and marriage deeply personal. It calls forth the possibility of extraordinary encounters that, in marriage, expect and embrace the fullness of love, spiritually, emotionally, mentally, and physically. This intimately personal view influences Bonetti's attempts to connect the symbolism in marriage with the everyday realities of marriage that I discussed in chapter 2. One of the critiques of Theology of the Body is that it oversells a lifelong expectation for a deeply personal and mysterious human-divine connection in every aspect of marriage.[12] It's not a bad critique. Life is mostly ordinary. But if we're living members of the body of Christ, it's okay to expect the extraordinary to break in as we saw with the *aha* moments. And while I don't need a holy and mysterious *aha* moment to happen every day, I know that some days it does—and when it does, I consider it pure gift.

Marriage is personal. It is a holy and mysterious image of a holy and mysterious God. It's also an ongoing education in dignity and basic human responsibility (doing the laundry, taking out the trash). Throughout married life we see unity in distinction at play. This is what the apostle Paul was getting at when he discussed the one body and the many parts (cf. 1 Corinthians 12; Romans 12). I can't make Carey be like me and she can't make me be like her. Instead, we learn to call out the grace operating in one another as we attempt (with God's help) to love one another unconditionally. Then we find unity—and power—in the distinct ways in which we operate and we allow those gifts to give life to one another and to the world.

Original Nakedness

In the beginning, man and woman were naked and felt no shame (Gen. 2:25). This level of vulnerability, safety, and security is foundational to the human experience.

---

12. See McCarthy, *Sex and Love in the Home*, 42–44.

"Indeed [these experiences] are so interwoven with the ordinary things of life that we do not realize their ordinary character."[13] If the relationship of male and female in marriage lived out through the family and in shared community with others is to mean anything, we must first understand the extraordinary nature of this statement.

In the beginning, nakedness symbolized an original good, an all-encompassing understanding of purity and wholeness of body, mind, and spirit. In this idea of nakedness, humans are fully exposed, fully vulnerable, yet feel no shame. It is to "see and know each other . . . with all the peace of the interior gaze, which creates precisely the fullness of the intimacy of persons."[14] This level of intimacy allows man and woman to become a gift for each other, embodying two diverse ways of being a body. Their act of mutual self-giving in the marriage relationship is a clarion call animating all other relationships. The act of self-giving is what John Paul II calls the *spousal meaning of the body.* Man and woman were designed to give body and life to each other freely, totally, and without shame.

While the fall of humanity distorted this vision of spousal love, Christ's ultimate act of self-giving through his death on the cross points the way forward. He has the ultimate victory over a distorted vision of love and sexual intimacy. We will not find ourselves, our identity, or our sexuality until we find our life in God. This requires admitting and seeking healing from our own guilt and shame so that we can freely give ourselves to

13. John Paul II, *Man and Woman He Created Them*, 170.
14. Ibid., 178.

one another. Only in the act of self-giving in the context of healthy personal relationships do we truly know who we are and how to express ourselves sexually. This is why families and family-like communities are needed more than ever before. In a culture charged with misbegotten notions of sex and marriage, family-like communities shaped by the cross of Christ become the places of safety, vulnerability—and challenge—where love is expressed in a pure and holy way. Original nakedness is a threshold moment. The call for us in this moment is to live as agents of God's self-giving love, with God's help, until God finally makes everything right.

These three originals provide a thoughtful framework for understanding our desire for divine and human relationship. We will see how the deepest longings of our bodies and our hearts are designed to pull us higher with Jesus leading the way.

My introduction to this stream of thought has become more clear through my study of Theology of the Body and began through a series of trusting relationships. In 2012, during our first year in ministry at the University of Mary Washington, Carey and I linked up with our colleague and friend Father Fred Edlefsen, the chaplain of the Catholic Campus Ministry, and gathered some university students for a discussion series on the first twelve chapters of Genesis. The prospect of Protestants and Catholics reading the Bible together generated some curiosity on campus. Each week a few students showed up who were pretty sure they didn't believe anything about the faith we discussed, but somehow they were intrigued. I think one of them even wrote an article about it for the student newspaper. A few in our group of mostly Baptist and evangelical-leaning students were especially intrigued when they figured out that the Catholic students knew their Bible better than they did. But that was just the beginning of what would unfold.

The following year, Tory Baucum, then chairman of the Fresh Expressions US Board, made several references to those early chapters of Genesis during his main stage presentation at the inaugural Missio Alliance gathering. I thought his remarks sounded a lot like Father Edlefsen, so when Carey and I asked him about it, Baucum introduced us to the work of Catholic writer Christopher West and later invited us to meet Monsignor Renzo Bonetti, the previously mentioned Italian priest.

In different ways each fitting their respective contexts, Baucum, West, and Bonetti had done the work of making the writings of John Paul II applicable to people's everyday lives. At the time, Baucum was leading a large suburban church. West founded The Cor Project, disseminating teaching and materials on the Theology of the Body in trainings offered around the world. Bonetti drafted family policy at the Vatican and eventually created the Mistero Grande foundation to replicate the domestic church as a way to strengthen the local parish church. Bonetti believed that families were key to bringing the gospel closer to people who had never truly heard it before. Through the foundation he trains families to adapt their homes and lives to the pattern of family-community evangelism we unpacked earlier. He engages married couples in counseling and training, teaches families to pray for their neighbors, and shows how married and family life works best when it is pulled out of the false reality of self-sufficiency and into community.

With the right posture and intention, Christian marriages, the families created by those marriages, and the friendships and community they inspire, are a way of being church. A closer look at the domestic church helps restore the church to a multigenerational model for life together as the family of God. While every person reflects the beauty of the incarnation, and marriage and parenthood aren't always a reality for every person, spiritual parenthood is the call of every Christian as a means of "[placing] the lonely in families" (Ps. 68:6). Home and family life provide a safe place for practicing healthy interpersonal relationships where we can be free from guilt and shame. As we've said, by reimagining the home as the first church and an extension of the local church, the home becomes a center for community and mission.

Jesus (God the Son) is the foundation for our understanding of community and mission. "The Son cannot be explained apart from God the Father and God the Spirit. He and all other persons operate in webs of relationships . . . because persons, human or divine, do not stand alone."[15] Webs of relationships in our own families of origin make us who we are. There are numerous resources and studies of family life and family systems theory. Knowing as much as we can about the experiences of our parents and the generations of our families

---

15. John Paul II, *Man and Woman He Created Them*, 170; Dennis Kinlaw, *Let's Start with Jesus: A New Way of Doing Theology* (Grand Rapids: Zondervan 2005), 80.

helps us better understand the role of Adam and Eve, our first parents, and the subsequent generations of biblical history pointing to Christ.[16]

When we know how our identity, our mission, and our purpose are shaped by God's love for every person, and as God's love shapes our relationship with others, we can appreciate the significance of married love as a visible symbol for the way God loves. As I've shown, this visible symbol of married love becomes inherently missional as every marriage is a family that, with the right focus and direction, reaches out to others, building the larger family of God.

Yesterday, after the little church gathering we host in our living room, we had just cleaned up from a Sunday lunch of take-out tacos. Carey, Becca (who lives across the street from us), and I were chatting when Matt and Holly, a young married couple in our community, rushed through the front door.

"We need to go and pray for my sister."

"Now?"

"Yes, now. She says there are evil spirits in her house. They are harassing her family and she is scared to sleep there another night."

This was not how I was planning to spend my evening. It was four o'clock and Matt's sister lives an hour away.

Several weeks earlier, Matt's sister and her family had moved into the farmhouse where Matt's dad grew

---

16. A good resource on this subject is: Peter Scazzero, *Emotionally Healthy Spirituality* (Grand Rapids: Zondervan, 2017), 71–96.

up. The house had been in the family for generations but had stood vacant for several years. Matt's sister and her family had decided to move in and were beginning renovations, but they hadn't slept much since they moved. They were fighting and arguing. There wasn't peace in the house. After a series of bad dreams and strange occurrences, they were scared and didn't know what to do. So they called Matt to ask for advice and Matt was ready to go right then. I wanted to make a plan and to make sure that if we went, we would be welcome.

Before long, Michael and Emma, another young couple from our community, and Wes, who lives in another house across the street, had heard the news and wanted to help. They all wanted to go pray for Matt's sister. So we made our plan. Matt called his parents and asked if they would be willing to meet us at the farmhouse. They agreed. His sister was tentative about our visit at first, but she also gave us the okay. I called my colleague Cheryl, the head of our Fresh Expressions prayer team. Carey called our friend Tim, then the interim rector at Truro Church, for his quick take on how to do a house blessing in an unsettled house. Michael went home and got his guitar. Carey packed Communion elements and a cross that hangs on our wall. Becca got her Bible. We prayed together for safety on the road and all eight of us—a little traveling church—made it to Matt's sister's house just before sundown. We offered prayers of peace in every room. We anointed the doorposts and the windows. We prayed for the children. We prayed for the generations who had grown up in the house. We prayed for healthy relationships and for a freedom from fear. We prayed for anything in the house or in the lives of the people who lived in the house that was not of God to go to Jesus. We were cool and calm. We didn't carry on for very long. We didn't want to give demons or whatever evil spirits that might have been confusing the situation more of our time and attention than was necessary.

After the house blessing was over, we went outside. I got out the Communion elements and the hood of Matt and Holly's car became a table. I thought about Karol Wojtyla and his makeshift altar on those upturned canoes. I prayed that the bread and cup would become signs of new and unending life in Christ. We shared Communion together. Then we sang "Amazing Grace." We forgot some of the words, but we kept on singing anyway. When we finished singing, Matt's mom said she could envision that home and that land as a gathering place for this and for future generations.

On our way home, we stopped for takeout and then the eight of us gathered around our dining room table. With paper plates and pizza in hand, we discussed all that had transpired that night. Michael got out his guitar and we all began to sing. As we did, Matt's sister sent a text saying how much more peaceful their house felt. The truth is that all of us felt peace and a greater measure of healing because of the experience we had just shared together.

Something we learn from Jesus' ministry is that he spent a lot of time eating and healing. This is the gift of the church lived out as a family on mission meeting up with other families on mission to build the great big family of God.

Questions for Reflection

- How might your family or family-like community make yourself available to build the great big family of God?
- Are you more prone to action (like Martha) or contemplation (like Mary)? How might your preferred way of operating become more aligned so that you become a gift able to see others in the same way?
- Think about what you most desire. How might that desire be given over and rightly ordered by the love of God?
- Think of a recent *aha* or *uh-oh* moment. What are you learning from it and how are you sharing that learning with others?

Little children, let us love, not in word or speech, but in truth and action.

—1 John 3:18 (NRSV)

CHAPTER
SEVEN

Even When It Hurts: The Economics of Gift

My friend Danilo is from Sicily. He and his wife, Alona, run the best restaurant in town. The place is always packed and it seems like Danilo is always giving something away for free. An extra cannoli here, a free shot of espresso there. At first, the freedom with which he gave made me feel uncomfortable. As a white American male who likes to keep my cards close to my chest, my cultural presuppositions made me question whether or not he was being genuine. As an Italian, his cultural presuppositions are quite the opposite. Where I am guarded, Danilo is disarming. Where my tendency is to cling to self-sufficiency, Danilo's actions show me how much better life is when we learn to receive a gift.

Gift and reciprocity are foundational to how Danilo and Alona understand their marriage. It's how they run their business too. Everyone who enters their restaurant is treated like a member of the family and they sincerely hope that others might do the same in their homes and workplaces. Sometimes their actions are reciprocated, sometimes not. But this is how it is in the economy of gift. *Oikos*, the word for household in Greek, is the root for the word "economy" (*oikonomia*). Oikos is also the root for the word "ecology" (*oekologie*). An understanding of both the economy and the environment starts at home.

As I shared earlier, the early church took root in households. The home served as the base of operations, not just for the family, but also for the business of the family and their associates. In 2020, the COVID-19 pandemic required home to become the base of operations once again. Suddenly we were working from home, educating from home, worshiping from home, and cooking every meal at home. While the pandemic brought great challenge and struggle and the loss of far too many lives, the reorientation of life around home gives us a sense of the idea of oikos, where the home is foundational to an integrated economic life. The challenge now is to carry the best of that experience with us even as we desire to leave the worst parts behind.

The great essayist and cultural critic Wendell Berry says that to be "uninterested in economy is to be uninterested in the practice of religion; it is to be uninterested in culture and character."[1] Berry pushes his readers to consider what kind of economy would be responsible for the holiness of life and worries that most of what he

---

1. Wendell Berry, *Sex, Economy, Freedom and Community* (New York: Random House, 1993), 99.

calls organized Christianity hasn't given the question adequate consideration. Our deepened understanding of home as the little church helps us address Berry's concern. I'm no economist, but if the early church met in homes and shared their goods in common, distributing their goods to those who had need (Acts 2:42–47), it's right and good to continue this line of argument to show how our theology of the household is also an economic reality.

From the outset I've called into question the idea of the self-sufficient marriage and the self-sufficient family. We've talked about the beauty and mystery of marriage within webs of relationships. This draws us to consider an economy rooted in gift.

In this paradigm—the economy of gift—there is an equal understanding between the role of the individual and the role of community in the free market. For the Christian, the idea of a free market is the ability to be "wrapped up in the will of God."[2] What if human transaction of goods and services wasn't our primary economic focus, but it was the idea of human cooperation instead? While some will accuse me of being naïve on this point, to have a view of economy that is wrapped up in the will of God is better understood through the lens of cooperation for mutual benefit that recognizes the person (the idea of reciprocity) than it is through the lens of transaction (an impersonal exchange of goods and services). For reciprocity to be commonplace, we must be willing to take up

2. William T. Cavanaugh, *Being Consumed: Economics and Christian Desire* (Grand Rapids: Eerdmans, 2008), 8.

our cross and walk a step further toward the idea of gratuitousness (an unmerited act). *Gratuitousness* is a word that needs some unpacking. It's most often thought of as something outrageous or uncalled for. We often think of it in the negative, as in gratuitous violence or gratuitous sex. In a more positive light, we might think of the gratuity I add to the bill after a glorious bowl of *Orecchiette bari* at Danilo's restaurant—which when not required for parties of ten or more—is a gift of *gratitude* for good service. In 2020, a news story about a waitress who received a $2,020 tip on a $23 tab caused a kind of grassroots gratuity challenge. People in the service industry from around the US posted pictures and told stories of the unmerited gifts they received from their customers.

If we continue along those lines, the word for an outrageous, uncalled for, and unmerited act becomes a powerful illustration that shows us how grace works. It's God's love for every person that informs our love for every person. I think this is what motivates my friend Danilo to give an extra cannoli for free. But here's something more:

> Significantly gratuitousness is not motivated by altruism, but by the intention of establishing an interpersonal relation. In such an exchange, in offering something to another I do so freely, gratuitously, without obligating the recipient to some form of return. In such direct interactions I will eventually be hurt by someone who betrays my offer, my gift, but if I can respond in gratuitousness, I can model and foster reciprocity in society. . . . It differs from the neoclassical economic view that focuses on the goods and

> services exchanged . . . [in this way] relationship with the other is the primary good; above all, that relationship must be preserved to live our lives to the fullest.[3]

To value people above products and relationship as the primary good, sometimes we have to give even when it hurts. Even when there is no reciprocity. But just as I hope that my marriage is an echo of the eternal mystery of God, I hope that somehow that same hope can lead others to an economy of cooperation where we focus on relationships and help each other become a little more human. The 2020 gratuity challenge is an example of gratuitous acts. These acts awaken us to the idea that every person in society can be a gift to others and can rely on others to be a gift in return.

Mutual giving and receiving is core to our humanity and it is core to our understanding of God's love. In his article "The Promise and Peril of Missional Entrepreneurship," British social entrepreneur Mark Sampson notes that this understanding of God and humanity is central to what he and others call the civil economy, an Italian economic model (ironically) "based on a relational anthropology that has its roots in Christian theology." This model "envisions a market economy saturated with gift and reciprocity, which serve to develop and

---

3. Luigino Bruni and Stefano Zamagni, *Civil Economy: Another Idea of the Market,* trans. N. Michael Brennen (Newcastle Upon Tyne, UK: Agenda, 2016), 76.

sustain rather than hinder human relationships."[4] Civil economic theory presents a hopeful rationale for holiness in the economy. It frees us to be gifts to each other.

Because God is love, his unmerited gift of grace resurrects this love in us. In the same way, love isn't merely something to understand with our minds; it is contemplation and action (see 1 John 4:8). Theologian John Armstrong wrote: "What we ultimately love gives us our sense of purpose and fills our life with meaning. That is, we think, not because we are, but because we are loved."[5]

Where Wendell Berry worries that Christians have failed to consider their role in economy, Armstrong worries that the church has drained the word *love* of much of its meaning and the rest of society has followed suit. The Christian understanding of love is not a box full

---

4. Sampson notes a similar theme in the third encyclical of Pope Benedict XVI: *Caritas in Veritate (Love, Charity in Truth).* (https://churchmissionsociety.org/resources/promise-and-peril-missional-entrepreneurship-mark-sampson-anvil-vol-33-issue-1) accessed June 12, 2018. An understanding of the household and family-like relationships is foundational for a renewed understanding of how we are shaped—and reshaped—by a market economy that values the essence of our humanity. Capitalism, Sampson argues along with Bruni and Zamagni, is but one part of a market economy that must take the development of whole people into account in addition to the development of free markets.

5. John Armstrong, *Costly Love: The Way to True Unity for All the Followers of Jesus* (Hyde Park, NY: New City Press, 2017), 7.

of chocolates or a heart-the-Instagram-post kind of love. Armstrong wants to scrub off that word so we might read it again and act differently. For Armstrong, God's love is a costly love. It's got flesh and bones, muscles and tendons. Costly love is exhibited through sacrifice. At the same time, costly love dares to enter our world in the most vulnerable form. Without God's free and undeserved gift to us, love is impossible. So is the economy of gift. Embracing a costly love requires a death—a letting go—and it's hard to let go when you don't feel the safety and security of love. By taking the world as we normally think of it and making something else, the family-community creates a secure environment. This environment becomes a different culture from the world we were used to.

Wendell Berry's novel *Jayber Crow* tells the story of the little town of Port William, Kentucky, through the eyes of the town barber. Berry has a unique gift for helping make our recent history and culture come alive. His descriptions of the changes in the rural economy in the time between the Great Depression and the mid-1980s provide a helpful illustration for the times in which we live today.

Up until the 1980s, many small towns had yet to see cable television or big box stores. People in small towns and rural areas still farmed a little plot of land where they raised chickens and other livestock as a vital part of the local economy. Berry argues that by the 1980s, the American economy had developed in such a way that it no longer wanted or needed people in little communities like Port William to raise their own food. Or to have chickens that produced eggs, for instance. The economy didn't need them to produce eggs, or eat eggs, it just needed them to *buy* eggs.

Some would argue that the US has produced the greatest economy the world has ever seen.[6] The American spirit that roared back after the Great Depression and helped win the Second World War created an elaborate supply system to get our troops abroad the supplies and rations they needed to win the war. Once the war ended, that same innovative system was unleashed upon the American population as a whole. As a result, mass-scale farming replaced many small family farms. Much of the food supply was processed in factories. Food became more convenient. Those who questioned processed foods and mass farming operations were thought to be on the wrong side of history. But history has a way of repeating itself. By the mid-2000s the farm-to-table movement began raising awareness about buying local and eating healthy. These new cultural realities are causing many to rethink food production and consumption. In many ways they're pointing us right back to the beginning. In some places people are becoming interested in the names of plants and animals again. We're learning about quality ingredients. Television programming; non-profit organizations like Martha's Table in Washington, DC; and local agricultural cooperatives are helping us become more aware of what sugar and fat and preservatives do to our bodies. The first humans were given stewardship of

---

6. It's also worth mentioning that the US also has the lowest savings rate of any wealthy country and is the most indebted society in history. See Cavanaugh, *Being Consumed*, 34.

creation and today, through local food and better nutrition, many are discovering the created order once again.

In his book *Culture Making*, Andy Crouch suggests that God gives humanity the task of "making something of the world." And this is the essence of culture. "Culture," Crouch argues, "is, first of all, the name for our relentless, restless human effort to take the world as it's given to us and make something else."[7] Like the disciples on the road to Emmaus, our eyes must be opened to the reality that the world has been fundamentally changed in Jesus. This is the hope of the kind of relationships established through the gift economy.

Still, the US is a consumer-based society. If we have money, we go to the store and we buy things. We absorb vast amounts of mass information on our personal electronic devices. Yet on the edges something new is happening. A few families in a post-war neighborhood in our city are producing eggs again. Several years ago, the city where we live passed an ordinance that allows every single-family home the right to keep and raise up to three chickens. So now Connie and Steve produce their own eggs. So do JoEllen and Zach. When our friends Phil and Kathryn retired and sold their house in a subdivision, they moved out to eighteen acres, where they produce more eggs than they could possibly eat—or sell. So, they give them to us for free. It's up to us whether or not we accept their gift. In a small way, their economy of gift is

7. Andy Crouch, *Culture Making: Recovering Our Creative Calling* (Downers Grove, IL: InterVarsity Press, 2008), 23.

taking the world as we normally think of it and making it into something else.

This economic analogy of chickens and eggs is yet another way of describing how God loves. God has more love than can possibly be consumed by God alone, so God gives love away for free, allowing us the freedom to choose whether to accept the gift of love and whether to give it away in return.

It's easy to see how this works with chickens and eggs. We can envision sharing fresh produce or yard tools with our neighbors; we can learn the stories of any number of monastic and other Christian communities who take seriously early church practice of shared possessions and the common purse, but how else might it work? I want to invite you to imagine how the oikos of the little churches might function together as the big church to build the big family of God.

Several years ago, Carey and I started leveraging our campus ministry center as a base for new enterprise. At that time, our facility, like many church buildings, was seldom used at full capacity. A group of local entrepreneurs was gathering on Friday mornings to create a start-up business development ecosystem for our region. Since some of them saw Carey and me as start-up ministry entrepreneurs, we were invited to meet with them too. When the group grew so large that we regularly broke the fire code at the coffee shop where we were meeting, we offered up our ministry space to the group.

Don, the owner of the coffee shop (a person of peace)[8], believed in what we were up to and started donating the coffee after we moved over to our space. Neil, the owner of a local doughnut shop brought breakfast. Those Friday morning meetings over coffee and doughnuts led the group to sponsor start-up business competitions hosted at the local community college. We created collaborative environments where entrepreneurs engaged in the regular exchange of ideas.

Will, one of the baristas at the coffee shop, launched his catering business out of our kitchen at the ministry center. The launch of the catering business earned him a down payment on a food truck, where he began serving Puerto Rican food like pork carnitas over tostones topped with a sauce that will make your mouth explode.

Carey got in on the action, too, partnering with three other local entrepreneurs to create the Good Turn Earth Company, a compost scheme for food waste. Every weekend she and her business partners got several loads of throwaway food from grocery stores and restaurants. Then they would collaborate with area youth agencies and local college students to compost the waste. The business was ahead of its time and needed significant capital investment to continue, but for a season they sold their product at the local farmer's market and at an area garden store. For Carey, it was a way to infuse her faith

---

8. A person of peace is someone who opens their home, resources, and/or relational network to you. A number of relationships in our lives were all brokered by Don. More about persons of peace in the next chapter.

with her understanding of economics and it was a way that she could be fruitful and multiply. The recovery of food waste into garden compost and the recycling of plastic food packaging that would have otherwise gone into a landfill was a compelling cause that invited even the most ardent skeptic to consider our partnership with God in the natural order of creation.

Some of the work from those years in the start-up community led leaders from our denomination to invest in a discipleship community for local entrepreneurs that Carey helped lead.[9] That's how we met Danilo and Alona. It didn't matter if these entrepreneurs were affiliated with our denomination, only that they were open to a leadership development process rooted in Christian practice. Over the first five years of the initiative, we cultivated relationships with eighty local business owners and their families. These business owners learned the power of the oikos as their faith, families, and businesses worked together in reciprocal friendship for benefit of our region. Some of these entrepreneurs considered ways that their businesses and the local church could partner to create investment funds for increased entrepreneurship. Some facilitated family-community evangelism or other forms of home-based worship. Some even started other ministries to reach out to their friends who might be done with church but not with God. In a day where people in business often *fund* mission and ministry, these business

9. This process is outlined in John P. Chandler's *Uptick: A Blueprint for Finding and Forming the Next Generation of Pioneering Kingdom Leaders* (Cody, WY: 100 Movements, 2019).

leaders learned how to be on mission at home, at work, and everywhere in between.

This little community of entrepreneurs may not have changed the direction of the US economy, but they learned how to integrate their faith with their work. They pushed back against the idea of self-sufficiency and they chose collaboration over competition. They are a courageous example of those who make the kind of economy that is also responsible for the holiness of life. And they learned how to see how their oikos points back to God, who holds nothing back in his quest for love. God gives creation to us and asks us to share in it. To name it. To steward it. This is how God designs us to make something of the world. God in Christ Jesus took on human flesh, giving all of himself to the point of agony and death so that his life could unite with our life. God's love moves us from passive consumerism to active participation in God's rule and reign. Once we have a taste of this union with him, we can't help but give our love away for God's sake and for the sake of others.

Some of us know people like my friends Danilo and Alona. Others will remember the kind of rural life depicted in Wendell Berry's little fictitious town where most everyone produced something and where capital was a lot more than money—because no one had very much money anyway. As American society has developed, we've come to understand an economy based almost entirely on the transaction of money for goods and services. Sadly, this view has shaped our understanding of God as well. Whether we're aware of it or not, some of us have grown up thinking that God's love is a kind of transaction or something we earn. Or it's something to consume as a passive observer in a church meeting rather than something we receive so that we can learn to give it away freely and joyfully without any reservation at all.

Yet, around the world something new is happening. Families are rediscovering the oikos. Local churches are doing the same. Local entrepreneurs are building community and raising their families together. Consumers are demanding socially responsible businesses and goods. Countries are beginning to look at personal happiness and not just gross domestic product. Local communities are relying more and more on local farmers and produce. We're crowdsourcing and crowdfunding enterprise.

The family-community is a natural place where the gift economy can be reimagined and lived out in big and small ways. In the family, we learn how mutual relationships of the sort that began with God's invitation to steward creation extend into friendships in every facet of life. Remember, it's not good for us to be alone. Our life together helps us live gratuitously. The gift economy of the oikos that creates healthy families and neighborhoods is yet another way of learning how to love like God loves.

Questions for Reflection

- Wendell Berry pushes his readers to consider what kind of economy would be responsible for the holiness of life. How do your economic practices shape your desire for holiness?
- How is your household/oikos functioning as your base of operations within a web of other relationships? How is your household engaging with other households to share more things in common?
- Think about fundraising, marketing, or other necessary components of doing business. How might your dealings with others develop personal relationships that are mutual and gratuitous (in the best sense)?
- Some Christian entrepreneurs consider it their mission to fund mission or ministry endeavors. This can develop a transactional relationship between the funder and those receiving funds. Instead of solely funding transactional ministry projects, how might Christian entrepreneurs or investors learn to become missionaries and how might missionaries learn to become entrepreneurs?

"Ask, and it will be given you; search, and you will find; knock, and the door will be opened for you."

—Matthew 7:7 (NRSV)

CHAPTER

EIGHT

The Way Home: How the Story of Jesus Shapes Our Body

God is distinct. Wholly other. Separate from creation yet involved in it. Humans are different. We're unified beings. We're emotional, spiritual, intellectual, and physical, but none of these attributes can exist without the others. The heart is the seat of our emotion. It's where all our capacities join together. The heart brings unity to our distinctives as people created in the image of God. This is why Jesus appeals to the heart.

Carey was born with two heart conditions—a mitral valve prolapse and a bicuspid aorta. The mitral valve prolapse required surgery. Carey processes emotions deeply, connecting with the pain and suffering of others in a way that I do not. Deep emotional connection is a special gift shared by people who've had a heart operation. Emotions come to the surface more often than they did before they had the surgery. When they're aware of this, and the reason for it, they can offer this gift to the world. They can offer the gift because they were quite literally cut to the core of their emotion. That kind of emotion, which for many of us is hidden, has come to the surface because of the unity between the physical act of heart surgery and the deep emotions that arise from the heart itself. The physical act of heart surgery serves as a metaphor for how our way home in Jesus is shaped by the condition of our heart.

Christopher West oversees The Cor Project. *Cor* is the Latin word for "heart." His project is committed to reframing our questions of human existence to show how God's love is imprinted on every person. He argues that our bodies are designed to reveal and proclaim God's love. West contends that God's love is the heart of the faith, and he laments that arguments around doctrine and interpretation crowd our understanding of the reality of God's love. He notes that many Christians haven't been taught to express the beauty and mystery of the image of God that is placed within and upon them—the theology deeply embedded within human biology and connected through the human heart and soul. West's work revolves around the application of John Paul II's Theology of the Body, noting that unless Christians understand the image of the gospel imprinted on our bodies and in our yearning for union with others, our efforts at evangelism will be greatly hampered.[1]

We need to look no further than the Christian story to see how this concept can be applied. It's a story for

---

1. Christopher West, *Theology of the Body for Beginners* (West Chester, PA: Ascension, 2009), 129.

every nation, tribe, and tongue. It knows no linguistic bounds. That story is so deeply connected *to* the body that we might even go as far as to say that the language of Christianity *is* the language *of* the body. Jesus is born, has died, and is risen in a body. The church is called the body of Christ. The concept of the body helps us articulate the hope we have in Jesus because Jesus is the Word made flesh (John 1:14). When we begin reading the story of Scripture through the lens of the body and person of Christ, we notice this sort of language everywhere and become better at comprehending what Jesus meant when he told his followers they would be known by the way they love each other (John 13:35). Love is the heart of the gospel. As followers of Jesus in a world disconnected from the story of Jesus, we will tell the story through our bodies and through our lives. Our lives show others how to know who Jesus is. We're the only Bible many will ever read.

Reading the Bible by Starting with Jesus

Sometimes I find that people go to the biblical text hunting for answers to the problems they face rather than looking for the mystery of love. They lift verses out of context to support their argument, taking poetry and parable and feeding it through a modern mental model as though the Bible were a kind of textbook that can be analyzed using the scientific method. But the Bible isn't a science book. It's a love song. It tells the story of Israel and how Israel, through Jesus, changes the world. It's not an abstract concept. It's intimate. Reading the text requires a fully engaged intellect, to be sure—but for Scripture to carry its full weight, the brain and the heart and the hands and the feet must all be fully engaged.

I like a good hypothetical biblical discussion just as much as anyone, but if we're not careful, we'll make God out to be an object of our discussions rather than the object of our affections. Is God sovereign? Does God choose us? Do we choose God? Why does God allow this or that or the other? While discussions *about* God are important, they sometimes miss the essence and beauty of the Christian witness. Instead of starting with doctrinal discussions or scientific debate, our invitation into the mystery of love is helped by beginning our study of Scripture with Jesus. This invitation is nothing new. Here, the Wesleyan theologian Dennis Kinlaw will be a helpful guide.[2]

In Luke 10, Jesus sends out seventy-two people just like you and me. They go two-by-two into the surrounding towns and villages as a sort of advance team for Jesus' mission. When they get to a new place, they go looking for homes and families to welcome them and their message.[3] First-century homes in the Middle East were vibrant, open places filled with people and activity. Since families often comprised immediate and extended family and friends,

---

2. Dennis Kinlaw, *Let's Start with Jesus: A New Way of Doing Theology* (Grand Rapids: Zondervan, 2005), 27.

3. "Whatever house you enter, first say 'Peace to this house!' And if anyone is there who shares in peace, your peace will rest on that person; but if not, it will return to you" (Luke 10:5–6 NRSV). We often refer to those upon whom peace rests as "persons of peace." They are often the people you meet who are friendly to you and often introduce you to others in their network or neighborhood.

the inclusion of a few travelers and guests into the mix would have been commonplace. Jesus told the followers to stay where they were welcomed. He told them to heal the sick who were there and to announce the kingdom of God in their midst. When these seventy-two normal, everyday people returned to Jesus, they were amazed at what his instruction enabled them to accomplish. They said that "even the demons submit to us in your name" (v. 17).

Jesus was overjoyed. Here we have a people engaged in active participation with God in creation. This action put the serpent we read about in Genesis back in his proper place. It showed the tempter who was really in charge of the world. The sight of regular people going out in faith and freedom on mission to the homes of complete and utter strangers gave Jesus great joy. He says that the works of the kingdom had been hidden from the wise and learned but had been revealed to these "little children" (v. 21).

What if we saw the childlike willingness of these seventy-two regular people as an echo of the original innocence of those first humans as they reflect the Father's love? The posture of their hearts, Jesus said, were for the Father's good pleasure. Jesus said, "No one knows who the Son is except the Father, and no one knows who the Father is except the Son and those to whom the Son chooses to reveal him" (v. 22). Through their actions in Luke 10, the followers of Jesus reflect the Father and the Son who are engaged in a constant state of giving and receiving love.

When I go to the gym with my friend Matt, he and I pass one of those weighted medicine balls back and forth. Over time, we develop a symbiotic rhythm and flow. There's a certain amount of trust involved. Matt passes me the ball, I receive it. I pass it back to him. Passing this weighted ball back and forth is a form of giving and receiving. Take this analogy, multiply it exponentially, and you'll have a glimpse of the relationship that exists between God the Father and God the Son. They are good at what they do together—but they don't keep it to themselves. They share the gift. In the same way, Matt and I often pray as we walk to and from the gym. We ask God to help us pay attention to anyone who might need help or a word of encouragement. This kind of dynamic, symbiotic relationship shows not just *that* God is love, but also *how* God is love. In order for love to exist, it takes two people who give and receive.[4]

In Luke 10, the love between Father and Son fuels the followers' participation in Jesus' mission and this thwarts Satan's plan. Satan thrives in chaos and confusion. God orders it. In Luke 10, Jesus rejoices at the love shown by these ordinary humans. He sees Satan fall from heaven (v. 18)! This illustrates the kind of new world created, ordered, and blessed by Jesus.

If you've seen a field of sunflowers, you'll recall how each flower follows the direction of the sun. Every flower is unified in their reception of light and heat. Sunflowers multiply through pollination. In some cases, sunflowers can self-pollinate, but this usually results in a deformed or unhealthy plant. Cross-pollination occurs when a third party—usually a butterfly, a bee, or the wind—moves the pollen from one flower to the next. The pollinated flowers then drop their seeds, resulting in more sunflowers. This metaphor is helpful for the way

4. Kinlaw, *Let's Start with Jesus*, 29.

we might understand the love that exists within God and how—through the wind-like power of God—we are cross-pollinated. Through God working within us, we drop more seeds, resulting in more flowers. This flowering or fruitfulness looks different for each of us, but in the best case it is the result of the creative energy of God's love working in and through us.

John's gospel is filled with these sorts of examples. In John 10 it says, "I am the good shepherd; I know my sheep and my sheep know me—just as the Father knows me and I know the Father—and I lay down my life for the sheep" (vv. 14–15). There's that symbiotic relationship again. Later, Jesus says that he and the Father are one and that we can *all* be one with the Father. Jesus then refers to Psalm 82 where it says that you (we) are gods (John 10:34–35; Ps. 82:6). This statement is immense. Jesus coming down to be with us and laying his life down for us is a difficult enough proposition, but we don't often realize the fact that, in Christ's incarnation, our humanity is brought into God. We are mortal. Subject to death, but not defeated by it. We cannot become like Jesus on our own, but because he gives himself to us. Saint Augustine said: "If by the word of God people become gods, if by participation, they become gods, can he in whom they participate [Jesus] not be God?"[5] The creed of St. Athanasius is based on Augustine's thought. Written in the fifth century, it says that Christ is both divine and human "not by conversion of the Godhead

---

5. *Ancient Christian Commentary on Scripture: John 1–10*, ed. Thomas Oden (Downers Grove, IL: InterVarsity, 2006), 363.

into flesh, but by taking of that manhood into God." Jesus has the authority to bring us into himself and in this is what gives us the authority to announce the good news of his coming. It is a radical and hopeful proposition and it does not come by anything we do on our own. It comes because of God's gracious gift and our choice to receive it.

In our church community, we distill the rhythm of life with Jesus and one another down to three basic moves: up, in, and out.[6] Up is our love of God. In is our love for ourselves and for one another. Out is our love for those outside our community—with a particular view toward those who think that they might not be good enough for God. Up, in, and out are all reflected in the Great Commandment in Matthew 22:37–39 (love the Lord your God with all your heart, soul, mind, and strength and love your neighbor as you love yourself), but the new commandment in John 13:34–35 (you will be known by the way you love each other) places a greater emphasis upon the in.

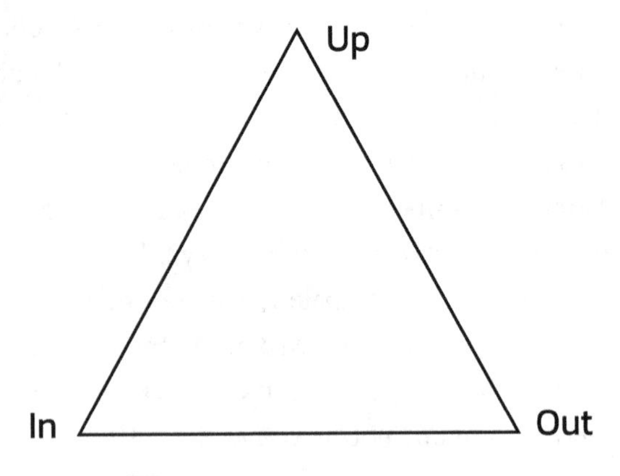

6. Mike Breen, *Building a Discipling Culture* (Greenville, SC: 3DM Publishing, 2016), 91–110. We're grateful for the work of Mike Breen, Paul Maconochie, and others for their insight.

Again, it starts with Jesus. The love that those who follow Jesus have for one another is a tangible sign of Jesus' presence in the world. Poetry attributed to St. Theresa of Avila (1515–1582) bolsters this point:

> Christ has no body now but yours,
> no hands, no feet on earth but yours.
> Yours are the eyes with which He sees,
> Yours are the feet with which He walks,
> Yours are the hands with which
> He blesses all the world.

Love is the hallmark for discipleship. It is the theme for our life as a gathered community of Jesus followers, but it only works if we share it. The Gospel of "John's emphasis on intra-communal love is often seen as a license for sentimental complacency . . . [but] God-love is never passive . . . we cannot hide in it and then write off the world."[7] The community of believers must boldly and faithfully bear witness to the power of the love within their shared life lived out toward others. Ours is a public faith, a witness to Christ's power and authority. We show this by allowing our desire for God to shape all of our other loves. As we saw with the sunflowers, God's love acts as a sort of spiritual cross-pollinator. If we acknowledge our desires and give them away to the wind of the Spirit, those desires are redirected toward Jesus, who intercedes before the Father on our behalf. We saw this in chapter 6 in the discussion of eros and agape love. This

---

7. John Armstrong, *Costly Love: The Way to True Unity for All the Followers of Jesus* (Hyde Park, NY: New City Press, 2017), 147.

is yet another mystery of our faith, but in as much as we are able to receive love from God, the Spirit refocuses and re-pollinates our hearts, increasing our capacity to multiply our life in our homes, communities, and relationships. This is the way God's love is made present in the world.

Jesus Shows the Way Home

In John 14, Jesus promises the gift of the Spirit and prepares the disciples for his departure. He's going to prepare a place for them. Thomas, the disciple who best personifies all of us who doubt the ways of Jesus, says, "Lord, we don't know where you are going, so how can we know the way?" (v. 5). Jesus' answer summarizes what I want to communicate. He says that Thomas *does in fact* know the way because Jesus is the way. Jesus shows Thomas (and all of us) the way home. "I am the way and the truth and the life," Jesus says, "No one comes to the Father except through me. If you *really* know me, you will know my Father as well" (vv. 6–7, emphasis mine). Once again, Jesus shows the mutuality of his relationship with the Father. He's acting in tandem, in total unity with him. With every action of the Father, there is the equal and opposite reaction of the Son. "These words you hear are not my own," Jesus says, "they belong to the Father who sent me" (v. 24). Jesus even says that anyone who has faith in him will do what he's been doing—and more (John 14:12)!

Many of us sign up for relationships without knowing where we're headed. It's like buying a bus ticket without knowing our destination. But Jesus shows us the road on which to travel because he is the way. Our relationships—when they're rooted in Jesus—help us get there. Our true destination—our heart's true home—is found in God. When we love God, God makes his home in us both individually and collectively. Again, the symbiotic relationship rooted in the giving and receiving of love is what stands at the heart of the Christian witness.

The Trinity's Relational Nature

The three so-called Abrahamic faiths—Judaism, Christianity, and Islam—are all considered *monotheistic*. Dennis Kinlaw suggests that it is Jesus who makes the difference between the monotheism of Christianity and that of Islam and Judaism because, in Jesus, we discover that the inner life of God is more than *bipolar*—it is *triune*. God the Holy Trinity lives in a continuous state of self-giving dialogue. "Understanding God as a Trinity of free persons gives us one of the most striking differences between the monotheism of Christianity and the other monotheistic religions . . . in Islam and Judaism God reigns without rival. He is alone, unchallenged."[8] Here, salvation becomes a reward for our obedience to the sovereign will of a sovereign God, but Christianity is more dynamic than this.

In Christianity, "the will of God is also supreme, but his will is conditioned by the interrelatedness in love of

8. Kinlaw, *Let's Start with Jesus*, 34.

the three persons that constitute the Godhead. The interpersonal context is crucial, providing an atmosphere of trust rather than mere external conformity and providing salvation as a gift of grace rather than a reward for one's good works."[9]

That interpersonal dynamism is known as *perichoresis* and shows how our personhood is received by our relationships with each other. This allows us to consider how marriage is an icon or image of the Trinity and the domestic church is an outgrowth of the mission of God. As the community of God—Father, Son, and Spirit—come alongside us in our own communities, we learn to love like God loves. As God the Holy Spirit fortifies our identity as members of God's family, we learn to see ourselves as children of the Father, and siblings and coheirs with the Son. The triune understanding of God helps us with three principal metaphors in Scripture that illustrate how God loves. These three metaphors are helpful tools to us as we proclaim God's love to the world.

The King and Judge Metaphor

If you were to approach a random person on the street and asked them to tell you about their image of God, you'd likely hear something about the big man in the sky. Press further, and you might learn that the big man sits on a throne or wears a long robe. The image of God that gets top billing in the minds of many is that of a king or a judge. The Scriptures, of course, are filled with these sorts

9. Kinlaw, *Let's Start with Jesus*, 34.

of images. Psalm 96 depicts the Lord who reigns among the nations as king and also as judge. Psalm 99:4 says, "The King is mighty, he loves justice . . ." In the Gospels, Jesus speaks often of the kingdom. He says the kingdom of God is near. He compares it to a mustard seed, a bit of yeast, and a pearl. He says the kingdom of God is within or among those who believe. The New Testament Scriptures conclude with John's vision in Revelation of the Great Judgment. There, it says: "the throne of God and the Lamb will be in the city, and his servants will serve him" (22:3).

God is both king *and* judge. This big-picture view of God is true, but it can be a difficult concept for us to wrap our minds around. Americans, for example, have more experience with judges than with kings. We fought for freedom from a king so it's the judge metaphor that has more often shaped the American view of God. This metaphor provides some context for the concept of *justification by faith*—a core doctrine of the Protestant Reformation. In this doctrine, humans are the lawbreakers who stand eternally condemned. It is Christ who takes the penalty for our sins, allowing us to stand redeemed in the presence of God.

The king and judge metaphor is important for our understanding of God, but it's not the only way of understanding. "If we view Christ's saving work only in terms of a legal change in status for the sinner, this handles the problem of sin's penalty but gives no answer to the *problem* of human sin."[10] Additional metaphors are

---

10. Kinlaw, *Let's Start with Jesus*, 50, emphasis mine.

needed to give a more complete picture of God's love. The Scriptures depict God as both king and judge, but they also show the covenantal reality of God as a family.

The Family Metaphor

As I've shared in earlier chapters, *family* is a loaded term. In the best cases, the word brings to mind happy memories of warmth, safety, and love. But it can also bring with it memories of pain, abuse, and neglect.

The kind of earthly relationships we have in our biological families inform our relationship with God. In the best cases, these relationships reflect the kind of relationship that Jesus shares with the Father. If this is the kind of relationship you've experienced with your earthly father, the world needs your experience and your voice! If you've experienced a difficult or nonexistent relationship with your father (or mother), extended spiritual family is often instrumental in redeeming that relationship. In times when our earthly family relationships seem distant, we need families with open arms who enfold others into their embrace. Families adept at modeling this show the way toward the kind of close and intimate relationship God desires with us.

It's not uncommon for us to describe one another as "God's children." I remember a conversation I had years ago with an older lady who reminded me that since we're all God's children, God doesn't have any grandchildren. What a thought! We're all God's children and our full identity is given to us through one particular people—the biblical people of Israel. In Exodus 4:22, God calls Israel his *firstborn* son. Through Israel, God promises to bless all the peoples of the earth.

In Scripture, Israel asked for a king and God granted their request. God allowed Israel to set up the institution, but families were God's idea from the very beginning. This may be the reason why families were foundational for the organization of the early church. Romans 16:3–5 says, "Greet Prisca and Aquilla, who work with me in Christ Jesus . . . greet also the church in their house" (NRSV). Philemon 1:1–3 says, "To Philemon, our dear friend and co-worker, to Apphia our sister to Archippus our fellow soldier, and to the church in your house: Grace to you and peace from God our Father and the Lord Jesus Christ" (NRSV). First Corinthians 16:19 says, "The churches of Asia send greetings. Aquila and Prisca, together with the church in their house greet you warmly in the Lord" (NRSV). This gives us a basis not only for the development of the early church in the home, but also shows a model for church led by both men and women.

God put all of us in families and "intended that those families should image the inner life of God himself and serve as a pedagogical device that could better enable us to understand the intimacy he seeks with us."[11] The word *pedagogy* is used to describe a method or process of education. It's the way a teacher arranges a classroom, or the principle orchestrates curriculum. In formal school, the pedagogy is explicit. In families, it is often implicit. In chapter 3 we showed how families are a sort of school for

---

11. Kinlaw, *Let's Start with Jesus*, 55.

life designed to teach us how to relate with and love one another in the ways that God loves. There is a pedagogy at work in every family that teaches us how to share (or not), how to clean our room (or not), how to feed the dog (or not). When the pedagogy works well, God's love can be proclaimed through webs of families and family-like relationships. For God's love to be present in this way, it takes families courageous enough to expand their understanding of family beyond the self-sufficient nuclear family with two kids, a dog, and a white picket fence to encompass *anyone* who needs family. In this way, they begin to see and experience the familial love of God—Father, Son, and Spirit—through the love of the family. When they do, those receiving the love of family might also begin reaching out to create family wherever they go.

Renzo Bonetti has said that "even the smallest family can build the family of God."[12] It doesn't need to be the best family. It just needs to be open to the fact that their life is a gift that they get to share with others. Jesus reorients and expands our views of family. When he is told that his mother and brothers are looking for him, Jesus responds by saying, "'Who is my mother and who are my brothers?' Pointing to his disciples, he said, 'Here are my mother and brothers! For whoever does the will of my Father in heaven is my brother and sister and mother'" (Matt. 12:48–50 NRSV).

The apostle Paul uses adoption language to show how Jesus reorients and invites us into a new family. In

12. https://freshexpressionsus.org/amore-plenary-session-descriptions/.

Jesus, he says, "we might receive adoption as children. And because you are children, God has sent the Spirit of his Son into our hearts, crying, 'Abba! Father!' So you are no longer a slave but a child, and if a child then also an heir, through God" (Gal. 4:5–7 NRSV). If we are heirs of the Father, we all are brothers and sisters of Jesus. This metaphor gives us a clearer understanding of how we are meant to do the things Jesus did—and that we're designed to do it together as a family.

The Nuptial Metaphor

The most intimate of all the metaphors, the nuptial metaphor shows the depth of God's desire to become one with us. It may sound odd, but God's intention is to marry us! Scripture begins with a wedding in a garden. Jesus—the bridegroom—performs his first miracle at a wedding. In the middle of the Old Testament, the Song of Solomon gives us a dramatic screenplay and beautiful soundtrack for the way that God loves:

> The voice of my beloved!
>   Look, he comes,
> leaping upon the mountains,
>   bounding over the hills.
> My beloved is like a gazelle
>   or a young stag.
> Look, there he stands
>   behind our wall,
> gazing in at the windows,
>   looking through the lattice.

My beloved speaks and says to me:
"Arise, my love, my fair one,
and come away;
for now the winter is past,
the rain is over and gone."
(Song of Solomon 2:8–11 NRSV)

Even when we stray or when our desires become adulterous, even when we fall far from the holy bliss that can only be experienced in our relationship with God, the Scriptures point us in the direction of nuptial love as that which far surpasses the typically cheap and counterfeit ways that we are often taught to love. Nuptial love calls us higher. It's sacrificial and self-giving. This higher way is difficult. It's all-encompassing. It demands much. Where counterfeit love can be sold as a thirty-day get-rich-quick scheme, nuptial love is a commitment that builds wealth over time.

The Scriptures give countless examples of how Israel exchanges nuptial love for counterfeit love. To illustrate the waywardness of Israel, God tells the prophet Hosea to take an adulterous wife. No matter how adulterous Hosea's wife is, he stays with her. "The marriage metaphor so permeated Israel's thought that it determined the Old Testament's usage of the words for *adultery* and *harlotry*."[13] Kinlaw notes that these words are just as often used to describe spiritual relationships as they are sexual ones. To describe Israel, the prophet Isaiah uses the words "Hephzibah" (married) and "Beulah" (promised land)

---

13. Kinlaw, *Let's Start with Jesus*, 58.

to show that Israel is not just any land; it is a *married* land. Of Israel, the prophet Isaiah says, "As a bridegroom rejoices over his bride so will your God rejoice over you" (Isa. 62:5b). Kinlaw says that the nuptial relationship between God, the land, and the people of Israel was so commonly understood that it was taken for granted by the New Testament writers to the point that it's not even explained! He takes an example from John 3:22–30 to make his point. When John's disciples became concerned that more people were going to Jesus to be baptized than were going to John, John explained his role. In today's language, John the Baptist would have been the best man in the wedding party. He's there to make the groom look good. "The bride belongs to the bridegroom." John said, "The friend who attends the bridegroom waits and listens for him, and is full of joy when he hears the bridegroom's voice. . . . He [the groom] must become greater, I must become less" (vv. 29–30).

When I got married, my best man, Brian, walked with me to the center of the aisle so that I could get a good look at my bride. When the time came for me to receive my bride, Brian got out of the way. Brian made me look good then, and he's still making me look good today.

The marital imagery continues throughout John's Gospel. In chapter 4, we read the story of the woman at the well. It contains within it all of the ingredients of a marriage scene. Jesus is at Jacob's well and he meets a woman there who had been married five times. He engages in conversation with her and eventually asks her for a drink of water. Jews were not permitted to interact with Samaritans. Both they and their water vessels would have been deemed unclean. Then Jesus reciprocates by offering *her* a drink of water—a radical action for the day. A man offering a drink to a woman was out of the ordinary. The fifth-century poet and church father Romanus Melodus wrote an allegory describing the woman as a picture of the church, and the well as the place of union with Jesus in the waters of baptism. At the well, the woman leaves her old life behind and comes forth from the water betrothed to the one true Master.[14]

The woman then becomes an unlikely evangelist as her testimony about Jesus causes many from that town to believe in Jesus—all because Jesus took the time to see her for who she really was. This is a good reminder for us. As we learn to see others as Jesus sees, he will draw them to himself.

In the Gospels, Jesus even goes so far as to use the nuptial metaphor to speak about himself. When asked why his disciples don't fast, he responds: "How can the guests of the bridegroom fast while he is with them?" (Mark 2:19). When the Pharisees challenge Jesus on marriage—saying that Moses permitted a certificate of divorce—Jesus says, in effect, this may be so, but at the beginning it was not this way (Matt. 19:4; Mark 10:2–12). Here, Jesus presents a new understanding of Scripture, making his case before the Pharisees by appealing to the beginning. Before the broken relationship between God

---

14. Romanus Melodus, Joel C. Elowsky (ed.) and Thomas C. Oden (gen. ed.), *KONTAKION on the Woman of Samaria 9.11–12, 14, Ancient Commentary of Scripture: New Testament IVa John 1–10* (Downers Grove, IL: InterVarsity Press, 2006), 157.

and God's people, there was a beautiful communion depicted in the relationship between husband and wife at peace with God and creation. We were all in. There was no hedging of bets, no looking for a less costly or counterfeit option. God was the sole object of our desire. The love expressed between God and people was reciprocal. It was holy and it was pure.

This is what we were made for. Despite our flaws, this is the future to which we strive. In the beginning, God saw that humanity was *very* good. In Jesus, the way it was at the beginning will be even better at the end. He is the way home.

Glory to the Father, and to the Son, and to the Holy Spirit. As it was in the beginning, is now, and will be forever, world without end. Amen.

—Gloria Patri

Questions for Reflection

- Dennis Kinlaw suggests reading the Bible by starting with Jesus. Does starting with Jesus reorient your scriptural imagination? If so, how?
- In Luke 10, Jesus deploys seventy-two everyday people to advance his mission. They go out to the surrounding cities and villages looking for people of peace. When they meet them, they eat what's given them and heal the sick who are there. What do we learn about Jesus' methods from this passage?
- Jesus does what he sees his Father doing. How do the three metaphors for God shape our view of God and inform our way of being a family on mission?
- The title of the book is *Bringing Church Home.* How does our understanding of Jesus as the Way shape our view of home up, in, and out—in God, in our bodies and family-communities, and out in the world?

Call to Action

The Fresh Expressions movement trains and equips people in every church for the opportunity to create church among those who the church isn't reaching. There are fresh expressions of church in community centers, restaurants, workplaces, schools, sports fields, homes, and neighborhoods. The hope of this book is that we will see fresh expressions of church emanating from our homes and the family-like communities that make up the (little) church.

To learn more about the movement or about how you can be part of it, go to FreshExpressionsUS.org.

Fresh Expressions is pleased to partner with a number of denominations, streams, and agencies within the Christian tradition who seek to give the inheritance of the faith to this and future generations. One of those partners is Live the Word, an initiative of the American Bible Society. Live the Word helps Scripture come alive through a better understanding of many of the practices addressed in this book such as radical kinship, empowered disciplemaking, participatory worship, and table fellowship. For more information on Live the Word, go to: www.LiveTheWordToday.com

CPSIA information can be obtained
at www.ICGtesting.com
Printed in the USA
LVHW010214190322
713651LV00006B/19